D1437360

FINANCE FOR NON-FINANCIAL MANAGERS

FINANCE FOR NON-FINANCIAL MANAGERS

R. VAUSE and N. WOODWARD

MANAGEMENT & MARKETING
BOOK CLUB

This edition published by
MANAGEMENT AND MARKETING BOOK CLUB
St Giles House, 49/50 Poland Street, W1A 2LG
by arrangement with THE MACMILLAN PRESS LTD

Typeset in Great Britain by
PREFACE LTD,
Salisbury, Wilts.
and printed in Great Britain by
LEWIS REPRINTS LTD
The Brown Knight and Truscott Group
London and Tonbridge

To NORMAN LEYLAND

The accountant wanted to be captain of the team, but they would not even let him play, giving him the job of scorer. So, in revenge, the accountant developed a system of scoring that no one else could understand.

Contents

Contents

Preface

The modern manager cannot for long escape the need to understand a financial report, whether it be the Balance Sheet of a competitor, an investment proposal, a product cost sheet, or a budgetary control report highlighting variances for the month. This book is written with the intention of providing a manager with sufficient grasp of financial and management accounting and allied subjects to enable him to make better use of the information available to him, and to see what information is relevant for the particular decision he has to make.

If, after reading the book, a manager is equipped to communicate with his accountant or financial adviser, and confident enough to do so, then it has succeeded in its intentions.

R.V.
N.W.

Oxford
December 1973

1 Introduction to Financial Accounting

Before a manager can really appreciate the various financial reports produced by companies all over the world, he has to understand the mechanics of financial accounting. The intention of this chapter is to explain the concepts and assumptions used by financial accountants in the preparation and presentation of financial information on business concerns. The concepts are, in themselves, straightforward and easy to grasp; the problems lie in their interpretation and application.

However, these concepts are important to any business, because their impact on the understanding and interpretation of financial reports is great. For example, how can a company show a healthy profit in its annual accounts, but go into liquidation soon after? This, as will be shown later in this chapter, can be explained by reference to one of the basic accounting concepts — accrual. Another question that often concerns managers is how the Balance Sheet actually balances; yet the mechanics of double-entry book keeping are based on a simple logical system.

There are two types of accountant that the manager will meet in the course of his work. First, the financial accountant, who is primarily concerned with the record-keeping aspect of company affairs, and with the presentation of financial results to management. The financial accountant and the auditor of the company attempt to provide an objective view of the financial situation of the company to anyone who has the right to see it. In particular, they work on the annual presentation of accounts, the Annual Report of the company. The financial accountant works within the boundaries of his professional body, within its rules, ethics and recommendations, as well, of course, as having regard to the relevant legislation applying to companies and their financial reports.

The second type of accountant is the management accountant. His main function is to assist management in decision-making activities. The management accountant provides managers of the firm with financial information that is relevant to their operations. This information will rarely become public property, and the management accountant, although using the same framework as the financial accountant, is not subject to the same legal and ethical constraints that pertain to formal reporting of company performance. He is concerned with the future, with trends, and with information for decisions and management control.

An apocryphal story will well illustrate the difference between the two types of accountants. It is of the managing director who advertised for an accountant. He had conducted a great number of interviews and had developed interviewing to its ultimate skill. He asked each candidate the same question. There were three candidates who had the necessary qualifications and experience, and each was asked the single question, 'What is one and one?' The first candidate, clearly a sound financial accountant, quickly replied, 'Two.' The second candidate was a bit smarter, and replied, 'It could be two, or it could be eleven.' The third, an experienced management accountant, answered, 'What are you doing, buying or selling?', and got the job.

The work of the management accountant and the assistance he can give to management is discussed later, but initially it is the work of the financial accountant that is studied, and the first step is to cover the fundamental conventions of accounting, and the concepts that accountants use in their work.

1. Accounting Concepts
Monetary Quantification Concept
It is axiomatic that a transaction or event cannot be translated into accounting terms unless it is capable of monetary quantification. If it proves impossible to put an event into monetary terms, the accountant cannot bring it into the accounts. The accountant is dealing with money

transactions, with the assets (things which are of value and owned by the firm) and liabilities (things that the company owes), and all are defined in monetary terms.

This monetary requirement for accounting is one of the sources of difficulty in the analysis and interpretation of accounting reports, particularly in the case of an attempt to value the shares or total worth of a business. There are many things which are of the utmost value to a company, but which cannot be accurately translated into money terms. The managers of a company, for example, never appear as either asset or liability in the accounts of a company. There has been some recent work on this subject of putting people in the Balance Sheet, but as yet it has still to gain widespread acceptance of real practical feasibility.

Business Entity Concept
When preparing a set of accounts, the financial accountant works on the legal assumption that the company has a separate identity from the people that make the company function — the managers, shareholders, directors and other employees. A company is assumed to have a 'corporate personality' and to have of itself rights and obligations independent of those who work in the company. A company can sue in its own name, and be sued, a company can also enter into a contract which is binding, as for example when the directors have service contracts.

The continued existence of the company is not normally affected by the death or dismissal of one of its directors, although clearly a 'one-man' company may be forced to cease trading under this situation.

Even when a company is owned and run by the same people, the business entity concept holds good. One of the earlier cases on this subject was *Salomon* v. *Salomon & Co. Ltd* (1897), where it was held that the company must be treated as a separate identity even when the major shareholder is also a key director. The result of this ruling was that the director who had made a secured loan to the company could still rank preferentially (be paid out before) to the other creditors of the company, even though that director held the majority of the company's shares.

It may seem that this concept has little to do with financial accounting beyond defining the legal corporate identity. But it does have a direct impact on the presentation of accounting information in annual reports. Indeed, it is this very concept that can be responsible for many of the problems managers have in reading accounts, particularly the Balance Sheet. It is this concept that necessitates any ploughed-back, or retained, profit to be shown as a liability in the Balance Sheet. This is because the 'company' owes to its shareholders the profit they have allowed it to retain, in just the same way as the 'company' owes them their original share capital.

Perhaps the most straightforward way to demonstrate this concept is to consider what occurs when a company is wound up. It is obvious that the company cannot retain any funds, for it ceases to exist. So these funds must be distributed. The company realises its assets by selling them for cash, and then distributes (pays out) this cash to its creditors (people to whom the company owes money for goods and services provided), and repays any loans that have been made to it. Finally, it gives the balance, if there is any, to the shareholders. The format of the accounts of a company reflects this process.

Going Concern Concept

In preparing a set of accounts for a business the accountant assumes that the firm is going to continue in existence for the foreseeable future, and that the business is not about to be sold or otherwise drastically altered.

This concept is similar to the next concept to be discussed; the cost valuation concept. For example, the accountant may know that a machine which the company owns could be sold today for £1,500 but it only cost the company £1,250 when it was purchased. If the accountant were trying to show the break-up or saleable value of the firm, he would use £1,500 as the value of the machine in the company's Balance Sheet. But as companies are not usually trying to sell out when they prepare their annual accounts, the accountant will fall into line with the going concern concept, and put the machine in the Balance Sheet at £1,250. He does this because it is impossible to predict accurately what will be the value of the machine when the company does actually cease trading, if indeed it does, during the lifetime of that particular machine.

Cost Valuation Concept

One reason for the use of the cost concept has already been put forward in dealing with the going concern concept, but there are other reasons why accountants use the cost of an asset as a measure of its value.

Cost is the only valuation which it is impossible to dispute. If a group of managers were asked what is the value of a particular machine in their factory they would probably all come up with different figures. What the value is will depend on the view taken. If the company cannot conduct its business without this machine, how is it to be valued? The managers might be asked about the replacement cost of the machine, and probably arrive at a different set of figures. Technological change may have rendered it obsolete, or less attractive, so that it would be replaced by a different model, and almost certainly the price of the machine will have increased since the purchase date of the original.

So when the accountant has to value the assets of a company, he uses cost as the basis. The accountant can produce irrefutable evidence of the actual cost of an asset — what the company actually paid the supplier. Whilst it is possible to argue that cost is not the best method to use in valuing the assets of a company, it is difficult to find any other form of valuation to substitute for it, or one which is as simple to operate.

An added incentive for using cost valuation is that depreciation allowances given by the government for tax purposes are all based on the historic cost of the assets concerned.

However, the problems which follow from the adoption of the cost valuation concept are considerable. For example, what happens when it becomes necessary to calculate the value of a business in a takeover situation, or to value the shares in a non-quoted company? Cost is clearly inadequate for this purpose because it does not truly reflect the current value of those assets. They may be worth more or less than the figure shown in the company's Balance Sheet. Indeed, by using the cost basis for valuing its assets a company can make itself a very attractive prospect for a takeover, by undervaluing the assets employed in the business. This can often occur with freehold land and buildings. There have been numerous cases of entrepreneurs seeing an undervalued company, buying it on the basis of the Balance Sheet valuations, and making a handsome profit by realising the true value of the assets after the takeover.

Realisation Concept

Accountants are often considered to be rather negative in their approach to the businessman's problems. They are very circumspect in what they accept from managers for accounting purposes. For instance, the accountant can never accept as revenue a sale until it has truly been completed with the customer. This is the realisation concept. The term 'realisation' here means that in the case of a sale the cash has actually to have been received by the company, or a clear legal obligation created for the customer to pay in the future for the goods or services that have been provided, before the accountant will take this transaction into the company's revenue statement.

If in November a company manufactures a batch of its products to a customer's order, and delivers them to the customer in December, the revenue, or sale, is not deemed to have taken place, as far as the accountant is concerned, until December. The mere manufacture of items against a customer's order does not in itself count as a sale, so if the company were to draw up its accounts in November the goods concerned would appear in stock, and not revenue. If, however, the accounts are drawn up for December, then the goods will be shown as part of the company's revenue in the Profit and Loss Account whether or not cash has been received.

Accrual Concept

In the final paragraph on the realisation concept it was stated that, whether or not cash had been received from the customer for the goods delivered, the transaction will be taken as a sale, and included as revenue in the Profit and Loss Account. This relates to the final concept to be covered here — the accrual concept.

It is this concept that can account for the fact that a company showing a good profitability in its Profit and Loss Account can go bankrupt soon after the accounts are produced. Accountants are not interested solely in the cash movement in the firm. In preparing a Profit and Loss Account the accountant is trying to measure for a given time period — normally one year — the revenues and expenses of the business. It does not matter, for the purposes of accounting in the Profit and Loss Account, whether or not the revenues or the expenses have been paid or received in cash.

Suppose a company purchases materials from a supplier and then, using those materials, sells the finished product to a customer. Even if the company has not yet settled the supplier's bill, these materials will be shown in the Profit and Loss Account as a cost against the revenue generated. In the same manner, if the customer has not yet paid cash for the products he has received, this will still be shown as a sale in the Profit and Loss Account.

It is thus possible in the short term for there to be little relationship between profitability and the cash generated by a company. A company which buys its materials on credit and sells on credit with a high mark-up can find itself in a cash crisis if the credit it extends to its customers is longer than credit allowed it by its suppliers. The Profit and Loss Account may show a very sound profitability, but there may be no cash in the bank to pay the coming week's wage bill, or a supplier demanding immediate payment.

1.2. The Duties of Accountants

As well as using certain accounting concepts, accountants also have a series of conventions which they apply in their work. The financial reporting period that accountants use is the calendar year — twelve months. The date upon which the annual accounts are drawn up signifies the date of the company's year-end. This breakdown of financial reporting into annual lumps does have certain drawbacks. There is no real reason to believe that this arbitrary time period gives the best information as to the real development of the company. However, in most countries the law demands that companies prepare at least annual accounts. This is often for tax reasons, as well as to safeguard shareholders' interests by not letting too long a period elapse between reporting.

Financial accountants are often seen as a professional body to be ultra-conservative or, less diplomatically, pessimistic when reporting company performance. Part of the reason for this has already been described in the explanation of the basic accounting concepts, but this pessimism can also be shown to come from, at least in part, the professional accountant's training.

The financial accountant must exercise a good deal of caution in order to avoid misleading those reading his figures. The auditor signs the annual accounts of a company as showing a 'true and fair view of the state of affairs'. He must be careful in the extreme, since others may take action on the basis of the information contained in the accounts. If the accountant were to mislead (and particularly to be over-optimistic) on a company's situation, then he would almost certainly be open to legal action by anyone acting on his accounts, as well as professional criticism for his actions. From management's point of view it can often be a nuisance to have an accountant who wishes to check and verify all their actions and activities, and to keep comprehensive records, but in this work the accountant is providing a very useful safeguard for all those interested in the company's affairs.

Accountants are often criticised for an apparent unwilling-ness to change their treatment and presentation of financial information. The reason for this consistency of approach is an important one, and reinforced by strict training. If accountants were not consistent in their treatment of the various expenses, revenues, assets and liabilities of the company, it would cause chaos for those trying to interpret and analyse company accounts. If the accountant each year changed the method of valuing a company's stock, to compare the past three years' performance of that company would be an impossible task since profitability as well as the assets would change as a result of the alteration in stock values. Thus, there would be no common basis for the analysis of financial reports; they would be non-comparable. This is why accountants are very reluctant to change their treatment of the various items incorporated into the annual accounts of a company. If they do change, then there will be notification of the change by way of note in the accounts.

One of the duties of the financial accountant is to maintain a strict record of all the assets and liabilities of a company. But there are, of necessity, limits beyond which the accountant should not go. There would be very little sympathy for the accountant who measured the length of unused pencils in the company offices so as to record these as an asset at the year-end. Not only would such a course of action be impracticable, but it would also be of little value in analysing that company's performance or financial stability. The accountant concerns himself only with material facts, and tries to produce only relevant information. With the case of the unused pencils, the accountant would probably just treat the total amount of pencils purchased as an expense in the Profit and Loss Account, without further analysis.

The Functions of the Auditor

The financial accountant reporting to the world at large on the activities of a business is expected to be completely objective in his work. This follows from what has been mentioned previously about the concepts and conventions, but it is worth emphasising this point because it is vital to the understanding of financial reports.

The auditor, the professional financial accountant who will sign the company's accounts as being a good representation of the state of affairs, is employed by the shareholders of the company. He is not employed by the directors of the company, except, obviously, where the directors are also the major shareholders of the company. The auditor's duties are closely defined both by statute and case law, as well as by the professional code of the institute of which he is a member.

The auditor prepares his report for the shareholders of the company, and as the shareholders cannot themselves be expected to check the records of the company, he undertakes this task for them. To enable the auditor to carry out his responsibilities fully, he is to some extent protected from management pressure by the fact that he cannot be summarily dismissed by the directors of a company without being offered the right to put his case to the shareholders concerning the conflict between the directors and himself.

The exact duties of the auditor are often misunderstood, and this can lead to a false sense of security when looking at a set of accounts which have been signed by a professional firm of accountants. The auditor is expected to use his professional skills to the full and to follow the various rules and regulations relating to company accounts. The auditor is basically concerned with the record-keeping of the company. Does the Profit and Loss Account adequately show the revenues and expenses of the company for the period covered? Are the assets and liabilities correctly listed in the Balance Sheet in a manner which meets his professional approval? To ensure that this is the case, the auditor must collect sufficient information, and check it for accuracy, so as to enable him to present his findings to the shareholders of the company in the required manner.

But there is no burden on the auditor to prepare the accounting data necessary to produce the accounts. This is the responsibility of the company's own accountants. The auditor is ordinarily there only to check the adequacy and accuracy of the company's internal record-keeping.

The auditor is not required to make any comment on the management of the company as to whether it is, in his opinion, good or bad, unless it directly relates to the presentation of the information to the shareholders in the Annual Report. A case where the auditor could be expected to make comment is where he finds that the company has not been maintaining adequate records of its trading, which makes it difficult to ensure the accuracy of the Profit and Loss Account or the amounts owed to or by the company.

The auditor is not expected to give advice to the management of the company in the running of their business. He may offer advice on the accounting system operated by the company, but even here there is no statutory obligation on him to do so.

The discovery and prevention of fraud is often assumed to be a prime objective of the auditor. But this is not the case. The auditor has no direct responsibility for this. Fraud is a matter for the management and accountants employed by the company.

Thus, the auditor is mainly concerned with the presentation of financial information in the legally defined manner to shareholders of the company, and little else. However, the majority of auditors who are professionally trained competent accountants do take their duties beyond the required minimum, and offer assistance to management wherever possible. Many of the larger firms of professional accountants are able to offer through separate departments the full range of management services and consultancy advice.

It is difficult to state categorically how far the auditor must concern himself with the use made of the accounts of a business once he has signed them. The case of *Chandler* v. *Crane Christmas & Co.* (1951) indicates that, as far as the law is concerned, the auditor has no duty to third parties who use his signed accounts. On the other hand, the more recent case of *Hedley Byrne & Co. Ltd* v. *Heller & Partners Ltd* (1963), though not a case dealing directly with accounting matters, does have a bearing on the current position of the auditor. The outcome of the Hedley Byrne case would appear to suggest that accountants preparing and signing accounts may find themselves liable to third parties if they have been negligent, though this has as yet to be tested in law.

1.3. The Mechanics of Basic Accounting

Many managers are put off by the apparently complicated and mysterious system of book-keeping, and so tend to shy away from studying accounting reports. However, as with any subject, unless the basic fabric has been understood there is little to be gained from advanced work. It is pointless to attempt meaningful analysis of an accounting report unless the manner in which a set of accounts is prepared has been mastered. This does not mean that the manager must become a trained accountant. The illustrations in this chapter are simple, and will not enable the manager either to maintain a set of accounting records or to prepare his own accounts.

Anyone requiring this competence should tackle any of the numerous books available on basic accounting or book-keeping.

Double-entry book-keeping appears to have been 'invented' towards the beginning of the fourteenth century. The name most often associated with it at this period in history is that of Paccioli, who wrote on the subject of record-keeping in Italy and, as an itinerant mathematics teacher, also devoted some time to gambling and probability analysis.

The basic concept of double-entry book-keeping is simplicity itself. It is that every transaction to be recorded shall have two entries in the books of account.

To illustrate the process of double-entry book-keeping in connection with the preparation of a set of annual accounts, assume that two brothers, John and Ben, decide to set up a small company to manufacture a product John has invented. Between them they have £5,000 with which to start the venture. Their first action, having formed a limited company, is to open a bank account for the company, and to pay into it the £5,000. The company is now in existence and must maintain records of transactions being undertaken. Working from the Cash Account of the company, the first entry would be:

CASH ACCOUNT

1 Jan. Capital introduced   £5,000

What has been done is to enter on the left-hand side of the page which is to record the company's cash transactions the fact that £5,000 has been paid into the account to start the business. However, this is only a single entry, and to fulfil the requirement of double-entry book-keeping a further entry is required. This would be:

SHARE CAPITAL ACCOUNT

1 Jan. John and Ben, cash introduced £5,000

A second account has been opened to record the fact that John and Ben have provided the initial capital of the company. In the case of the second entry in the Share Capital Account, the figure has been placed on the opposite side of the page to the one appearing in the Cash Account. This reflects the simple rule that all cash coming into the business is shown on the left-hand side of the Cash Account, and cash going out will appear on the right-hand side of the Cash Account. This can provide the basis for completing the other accounts in the records of the company.

The rule concerning two entries for each transaction can be restated as: whatever has been put on the left-hand side of an account, an equal sum must be entered on the right-hand side of another account. This has been followed in the two entries above: one on the left, and one on the right. The initial transaction, or movement of cash, to set the company up has been completed with the two entries in the books of account.

The next step for John and Ben is that they purchase ior cash a machine with which to manufacture their product, and pay the first month's rent on the workshop they are to use. These transactions are recorded in the Cash Account as:

CASH ACCOUNT

1 Jan. Capital introduced	5,000	5 Jan. Machine purchased	3,600
		7 Jan. January rent paid	100

The second entry relating to each of these cash outflows for the company is made:

MACHINE ACCOUNT

5 Jan. Cash paid	3,600

RENT ACCOUNT

7 Jan. January rent paid	100

For each type of transaction a new account is opened and used to complete the double-entry book-keeping process. It can now be seen that if the mechanical process of book-keeping with double entry is maintained without error, at any stage of the year the books of the company will be in balance. Or, to put this another way, at any stage the total of all the entries on the left-hand side of all the accounts will equal the total of all the entries on the right-hand side of all the accounts. Thus, on 7 January the position is:

Left-hand side		*Right-hand side*	
Cash Account	5,000	Share Capital Account	5,000
Machine Account	3,600	Cash Account	3,700
Rent Account	100		
	£8,700		£8,700

The total of all entries on the left-hand side is £8,700, and this balances with the £8,700 appearing for the right-hand side entries. It is this fact that is at the heart of book-keeping and, as will be shown later, enables the Profit and Loss Account and Balance Sheet to be drawn up with a minimum of trouble.

The company, having installed the machine, purchases some raw materials in order to manufacture a batch of the product ready for sale. A supplier agrees to deliver the raw materials on the understanding that his bill is settled within thirty days for the full amount of £800. The materials are delivered to the company's workshop, and there now exists an obligation on the company to pay the supplier £800. The company has also obtained an asset — the raw materials which it can use in production. These two facts make up the two sides of the entries in the company's books:

RAW MATERIALS ACCOUNT

10 Jan. Delivered by XYZ Ltd £800	

CREDITORS ACCOUNT

	10 Jan. XYZ Ltd £800

Two new accounts have been opened: one to record the asset, raw materials; the other to record the obligation, or liability, that the company has incurred to pay the supplier XYZ Ltd for the goods delivered. When the company pays the supplier there will be two entries to record this fact. The one will be placed on the right-hand side of the Cash Account to record the payment of £800, and the other on the left-hand side of the Creditors Account to show that the company no longer owes the supplier any money.

A simple series of rules can be developed to show how any transaction a company undertakes should be recorded:

A. Cash paid out and the obligation to pay out cash in the future are recorded on the right-hand side of the appropriate account.
B. Cash paid in, and the increase in the assets owned by the company, are recorded on the left-hand side of the appropriate account.
C. Expenses that the company incurs are entered on the left-hand side of the appropriate account.
D. Revenues or other income that the company produces are entered on the right-hand side of the appropriate account.

If these four simple rules are checked against the entries made for John and Ben, they will be seen to have been followed throughout. Note that cash paid out is distinguished from expenses, and cash paid in distinguished from revenues.

Next, the company manufactures a batch of its product, and sells it to customers in the locality. All the raw materials from XYZ Ltd are used up in producing sales of £1,900. The Sales Account is shown below and, following Rule D given above, the revenue is shown on the right-hand side of the account:

SALES ACCOUNT

	20 Jan. To various customers 1,900

By the end of January the company has received £1,200 in cash from customers, and is still owed £700 from firms John and Ben are certain will pay within the following month —

there are no bad debts likely. To record these debtors a new account is used and, as debtors are an asset to the company, the entry is placed on the left-hand side of the account. This is just the reverse of what was done in the creation of the Creditors Account.

DEBTORS ACCOUNT

30 Jan. Various customers	£700

The £1,200 that the company has received in cash for sales will have been entered into the left-hand side of the Cash Account. Thus, there is £1,900 appearing on the right-hand side of the Sales Account, and this is balanced by £1,200 on the left of the Cash Account, and £700 on the left of the Debtors Account.

If the transactions detailed above conclude the activity of the company in the first month of operations, it is possible to draw up a Profit and Loss Account and Balance Sheet to record the results. The first step in this will be to balance off each account. The Cash Account will now appear as:

CASH ACCOUNT

1 Jan. Capital introduced	5,000	5 Jan. Machine purchased	3,600
20 Jan. Sales to customers	1,200	7 Jan. January rent paid	100
		30 Jan. Heat and power paid	200
		31 Jan. Balance carried down	2,300
	£6,200		£6,200

31 Jan. Balance brought down 2,300

There are two entries in the Cash Account that require further explanation. The payment for heat and power covers the first month of the company's operations in the workshop, and was paid over to the landlord on the last day of the month. A separate account will have been opened to record this transaction, an expense to the company. The balance that exists in the Cash Account is £2,300; this is the amount of cash that the company has on 31 January. To balance off the account on the last day of the month, this amount must be added to the right-hand side, and it is brought down in the account to start off the records for February; this is done, as can be seen, using two entries.

Cash is clearly an asset to the company, and the Cash Account illustrates an extension to the rules given on page 15. This can be expressed as two further rules:

E. Assets of the company will appear as balances on the left-hand side of accounts.
F. Liabilities of the company will appear as balances on the right-hand side of accounts.

The Profit and Loss Account
The first stage in drawing up a set of accounts for the company is to draft the Profit and Loss Account for the period. This account deals with the revenue that has been generated, and with the costs and expenses incurred in the generation of that revenue. Throughout the production of the Profit and Loss Account the double-entry book-keeping procedure is maintained, but this time it is used to transfer items from their original account into the Profit and Loss Account. One entry is made in the original account, and the second entry, for the same amount, is made in the Profit and Loss Account. The completed Profit and Loss Account is shown below:

JOHN & BEN LTD

PROFIT AND LOSS ACCOUNT FOR JANUARY

(B) Raw materials consumed	800	(A) Sales	1,900
(C) Rent	100		
(D) Heat and power	200		
(E) Depreciation of machine	100		
(F) Profit for the month	700		
	£1,900		£1,900
		(F) Profit for month	700

To illustrate the process of preparing the Profit and Loss Account for entry (A) dealing with sales, the Sales Account would have had an entry made on the left-hand side:

31 Jan	To Profit and Loss Account	£1,900	20 Jan.	To various customers £1,900

This half of the double entry takes the sales revenue generated during the month out of the Sales Account; the other half entry (A) to the Profit and Loss Account brings sales into that account. The sales revenue for the month then has the expenses and costs set against it to determine whether a profit or loss has been made for the month. It will be noted that the total amount of sales is brought into the Profit and Loss Account, not just the £1,200 that has been received in cash by the end of the month. The Profit and Loss Account is dealing with revenues and expenses for a given time period, irrespective of whether they have been paid in cash at the time of the Profit and Loss Account's preparation.

Entry (B) in the Profit and Loss Account records the fact that £800 worth of raw materials has been used in the generation of the sales revenue. The same mechanical process would be followed to bring this amount into the account as was done with sales — except this time from the opposite side of the account because it is an expense, not revenue.

Entries (C) and (D) would be made in the same manner to bring the correct charge into the Profit and Loss Account.

Entry (E) deals with the recording of the depreciation of the machine. There should be an entry in the Profit and Loss Account to account for the use of the machine during the month, and to provide for its eventual replacement when it is worn out. Depreciation is dealt with in more detail in Chapter 2, but for the moment let a simple means of depreciation be used. Assume that the expected life of the machine is three years; using this, it is possible to assess how much depreciation should be charged in the January Profit and Loss Account:

$$\frac{\text{Initial cost of the machine}}{\text{Estimated life of machine}} = \frac{£3,600}{36 \text{ months}} = £100 \text{ per month}$$

To record depreciation adequately a new account must be opened, and the details entered in conjunction with the Machine Account:

DEPRECIATION ACCOUNT

31 Jan. Machine depreciation	100

MACHINE ACCOUNT

5 Jan. Cash paid	3,600	31 Jan. January depreciation	100
		31 Jan. Balance carried down	3,500
	£3,600		£3,600
31 Jan. Balance brought down	3,500		

The Machine Account has had depreciation charged for the month, and this is deducted from the original cost by the entry of £100 on the right-hand side of the account. This charge is taken to the Depreciation Account to complete the two entries necessary to record the charge. Entry (E) is made to the Profit and Loss Account, completing that account.

Having entered all the revenues and expenses in the Profit and Loss Account, all that remains to be done is to balance the account off. This is done by entry (F), which is the balancing figure necessary to make both sides of the account equal each other (£700). This shows that revenue has exceeded cost by £700, so the company has made a profit for the month of January. The balancing figure is brought down in the account ready for transfer to the Balance Sheet.

The Balance Sheet
The Balance Sheet of the company is set out below, and lists, as its name suggests, the balances existing on the books of the company on a certain day — in this case 31 January. This is all the Balance Sheet is. It does not attempt to show the value of the company, but to state in book-keeping terms the assets and liabilities of the company on the Balance Sheet day.

JOHN & BEN LTD

BALANCE SHEET, 31 JANUARY

Share Capital	5,000 (*d*)	Machine	3,500 (*a*)
Profit and Loss Account	700 (*e*)	Debtors	700 (*b*)
Creditor XYZ Ltd	800 (*f*)	Cash	2,300 (*c*)
	£6,500		£6,500

The left-hand side of the Balance Sheet lists the liabilities of the company on 31 January, and the right-hand side the assets on this date. If the double-entry book-keeping routine has been maintained correctly, it must balance.

To find the entries for the Balance Sheet, each account in the company's books is studied to see if it has a balance on it. If it has a balance on the right-hand side, then this is a liability (Rule F, p. 17); if on the left-hand side, this is an asset.

In the traditional U.K. Balance Sheet the liabilities are listed on the left-hand side, and assets on the right. This means that where a balance is on the left-hand side of an account, as with the Machine Account, then it is put on the right-hand side of the Balance Sheet – entry (*a*). This is a contradiction of the double-entry book-keeping rule as, by rights, a left-hand balance should appear on the left-hand side of the Balance Sheet. This method of reversing double entry at the Balance Sheet is peculiar to the U.K. and will not be encountered in many other countries.

Entries (*b*) and (*c*) are made in the same way as for the Machine Account, and when they are added together they provide the total for the right-hand side of the Balance Sheet (£6,500). If the books have been properly kept, it will be possible to find the remaining balances on the right-hand side of accounts that total the same amount.

The Share Capital Account shows a balance of £5,000 on the right-hand side, and this is entered on the left-hand side of the Balance Sheet as entry (*d*). This figure represents the amount that the company 'owes' to its shareholders. If the company were to go into liquidation, and the assets to achieve their stated values, this amount of £5,000 would be paid back to the shareholders; they would get their money back. As well as receiving their original capital back the shareholders would be entitled to the profit that the company has made. This is the balance on the Profit and Loss Account which is transferred to the Balance Sheet in entry (*e*).

The only remaining balance on the books of the company is the £800 appearing in the Creditors Account. This £800 is brought into the Balance Sheet by entry (*f*).

The accounts for John & Ben Ltd are now complete, and

all the available information has been extracted from the company's records. Clearly, in real life the situation would be far more complex, with many more entries and accounts being made in the books of the company, but this simple example does serve to illustrate the process that the accountant goes through when he sets about maintaining records for a firm, and preparing their accounts.

Debit and Credit

The system of double-entry book-keeping has been explained without reference to the terms 'debit' and 'credit', which accountants commonly use in their work. These terms have been avoided because they do not assist the non-financial manager in understanding the mechanics of book-keeping. Indeed, they only confuse the issue.

All a debit means is that the entry is to be made on the left-hand side of the account. Thus, if the Cash Account is debited for £5,000, this means that £5,000 is written in the left-hand side of that account.

Credit means the opposite of debit. If an account is credited, then an entry is made on the right-hand side of that account. Debit and credit are purely locational terms for the accountant. They have no other significance. In double-entry book-keeping every transaction must have a debit and a credit.

1.4. Balance Sheet Presentation

In the following chapters of this book the basic pattern of accounting will be expanded and developed to provide a fuller understanding of real-life company accounts. But before this is done, the actual presentation of the annual accounts of companies must be studied. With very few exceptions, companies do not provide a left-hand and right-hand side Balance Sheet or Profit and Loss Account. They still use the same process of book-keeping previously outlined, but in presenting their annual accounts it is ignored.

The basic building blocks of the Balance Sheet are shown below for a traditional layout:

BALANCE SHEET BLOCKS

Shareholders' funds (£5,700)		Fixed assets (£3,500)
Long-term loans		
Current liabilities (£800)		Current assets (£3,000)
(£6,500)		(£6,500)

The figures in brackets relate to the Balance Sheet of John & Ben Ltd, on page 19. Dealing with the liabilities side of the Balance Sheet first, there is the information as to whence the finance of the company came, or what the company owes. The first block relates to the shareholders' interest in the company. This consists of the share capital and the retained profits. The second block does not apply to John & Ben Ltd, and is for any loans that the company has received. The third block is the current liabilities; these are the short-term liabilities of the company. In the case of John & Ben Ltd they consist of the money owed to the supplier that will be paid out the following month.

The right-hand side of the Balance Sheet contains two blocks which show where the finance from the left-hand side of the account has been used — what physical assets the company has obtained through the employment of the available finance.

Fixed assets are defined as the assets that the company owns and uses to carry on its business. Thus, the machine that John & Ben Ltd purchased is a fixed asset; so would be land and buildings, if the company owned any. The second block is current assets. Current assets are items such as stock, debtors and cash that the company owns. They are distinct from fixed assets in that they will change quite rapidly as the company carries on its business. There will be a continual movement in the current assets of a company, and they should not be expected to stay static for long.

There is no statutory restriction on a company as to how it shall show the financial information in its annual accounts. As long as the information is there, it does not matter how it is presented, though there are certain acceptable means of doing this which financial accountants have developed over the years. Today most companies show their Balance Sheet as illustrated below. This is the columnar or tabular form of presentation.

All that has been done in this changed presentation is to subtract from both sides of the Balance Sheet the current liabilities (£800). The current liabilities block is taken from the liabilities side of the Balance Sheet, and shown as a deduction from the assets side. In most cases, current liabilities are deducted from current assets to show the net current assets or the working capital of the company. The use of working capital will be covered in Chapter 2 but, briefly, it shows that a company has more current — short-term — assets than it has current — short-term — liabilities. The company can pay all its current liabilities out of its current assets without having either to sell fixed assets or raise loans.

BALANCE SHEET BLOCKS

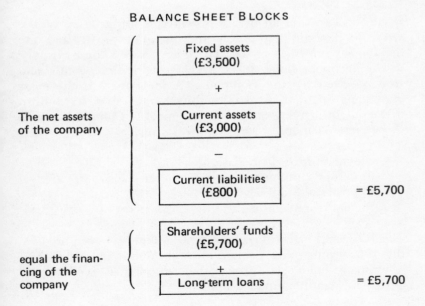

The total of the net assets of the company is £5,700. This equals the £5,700 of shareholders' funds. Instead of the longer-term liabilities of the company appearing on the opposite side of the page, these constitute the second change in the Balance Sheet presentation, by appearing underneath the net assets. In fact the Balance Sheet, still with exactly the same information in it, has been redrafted in a column. This is the format that is now commonly used by companies in their annual reporting.

1.5. Profit and Loss Account Presentation

Not only is the Balance Sheet presentation no longer made in the traditional left- and right-hand method. The Profit and Loss Account is also normally drafted in the columnar format. Companies do not have to show complete details of their trading operations, but only certain major items that are required under the two main Companies Acts (1948 and 1967).

To illustrate the form of Profit and Loss Account presentation followed by companies, we reproduce the Marks & Spencer Ltd Profit and Loss Account for the year ended 31 March 1972:

It can be seen that all that is provided is information on the sales of the company; pre- and post-tax profit; and the dividends paid or proposed. There are also on the next page in the accounts some notes which provide further information required by the Companies Acts. Note 2 is the most important in that it details the charges that have been deducted in arriving at the pre-tax profit. Companies must show certain expenses. The major ones are:

— the amount of depreciation
— directors' emoluments
— interest paid on loans
— the auditors' remuneration.

The information on directors' emoluments was required by the 1967 Companies Act and must show in bands of £2,500 how many directors receive that amount as well as the chairman's emoluments for the year.

PROFIT AND LOSS ACCOUNT, YEAR ENDED 31 MARCH 1972

	1971 (53 weeks)			1972 (52 weeks)	
	£	£		£	
Turnover—*Note 1*		416,685,000		463,022,000	
Profit before Taxation—*Note 2*		50,115,000		53,766,000	
Corporation tax—*Note 3*		18,900,000		19,350,000	
Profit after Taxation		31,215,000		34,416,000	
Stamp duty on increased capital		—		136,000	
		31,215,000		34,280,000	
Gross Dividends					
Preference Shares	105,000			105,000	
Ordinary Shares					
9¾% Interim Paid	7,136,000			7,877,000	
21½% Final Proposed	15,754,000			17,369,000	
		22,995,000		25,351,000	
Retained Profit		8,220,000		8,929,000	
Surplus on disposal of assets		2,393,000		203,000	
Undistributed Surplus		10,613,000		9,132,000	

The notes on page xx form an integral part of this Profit and Loss Account.

25

The only other details that are not self-explanatory in the Profit and Loss Account for Marks & Spencer Ltd are the stamp duty on increased capital — the amount that had to be paid to increase the capital of the company — and surplus on disposal of assets, which is the profit the company made on selling some of its assets.

The undistributed surplus of £9,132,000 is carried into the Balance Sheet to be added to the shareholders' funds.

2 The Analysis of Annual Accounts

In Chapter 1 the basic principles, concepts, terminology and conventions of financial accounting were introduced. These provide a basis for the analysis and interpretation of the financial information which companies provide in their Annual Reports. But first it is necessary to examine the information required in the Annual Report.

2.1. The Annual Report

Every company is required to provide a Profit and Loss Account (or an Income and Expenditure Account), together with a Balance Sheet, each year of its existence. This information must be presented to the shareholders, and others with a long-term interest in the company (e.g. debenture holders), at least twenty-one days prior to the Annual General Meeting of the company.

The 1948 Companies Act defines the information to be contained in the Annual Report, and this has been updated by the 1967 Companies Act. The general guide provided by the 8th Schedule of the 1948 Act together with Sections 147–158 gives the basis for all companies' reports. There is no particular layout or design of accounts prescribed by the Act. All that is statutorily defined is the information that shall be contained in each report.

The Annual Report must contain not only the Profit and Loss Account and Balance Sheet of the company each year, but also the Directors' Report. The contents of the Directors' Report are set out in Sections 16–20 of the 1967 Companies Act. In broad terms these are:

(a) A report as to the 'state of the company's affairs'. This is taken to mean a statement of the profit generated for the year.

(*b*) What dividends the directors are proposing for the year, and the amounts to be retained in the company by creating or adding to reserves in the Balance Sheet.

(*c*) A statement of the directors' shareholding in the company, including shares held by wives and children, and those held as trustee.

(*d*) A statement of changes in membership of the board.

(*e*) A statement of the average number of employees of the company and their total remuneration.

(*f*) Where the current value of land held by the company is substantially different from that shown in the Balance Sheet the directors must disclose this fact.

(*g*) A statement of charitable and political contributions made during the year — unless they total less than £50.

(*h*) The amount of revenue generated from exporting.

In effect, the 1967 Act broadened considerably the amount of information that a company is required to provide for its shareholders, and this process is likely to continue in future legislation, with more information being required for publication.

The Annual Report will also normally contain a Chairman's Statement to the shareholders in which he outlines the past year's operations and makes any comments he feels necessary. There will also be the Auditors' Report, which must conform with Section 149 of the 1948 Act, requiring that every Balance Sheet of a company 'shall give a true and fair view of the state of affairs of the company as at the end of its financial year'. This and the 9th Schedule of the 1948 Act constitute the typical Auditors' Report:

In our opinion the accounts set out on pages 00 to 00 give a true and fair view of the state of affairs of the company at 31 December 1973, and the profit for the year ended on that date, and comply with the Companies Acts, 1948 and 1967.

XYZ & Co.

15 February 1974   Chartered Accountants

Thus, a typical Annual Report can be expected to contain the following information:

— Directors' Report
— Chairman's Statement
— Auditors' Report
— Profit and Loss Account for the year
— Balance Sheet for the end of the year
— any notes that are required for full understanding of the Profit and Loss Account and Balance Sheet and necessary to comply with the 1948 and 1967 Companies Acts.

Often companies will provide further details of their operations in the Annual Report, but this is at their discretion.

2.2. The Balance Sheet

In the 8th Schedule of the 1948 Companies Act the broad outline of what the Balance Sheet must contain is given: 'The authorised share capital, issued share capital, liabilities and assets shall be summarised, with such particulars as are necessary to disclose the general nature of the assets and liabilities.'

To facilitate an understanding of how the various schedules of the Companies Acts are interpreted in real life, the 1972 Balance Sheet of Marks & Spencer Ltd is reproduced below. Marks & Spencer Ltd (hereafter referred to as M & S), although one of the largest companies in the U.K., has probably got one of the simplest Balance Sheets. It follows the format illustrated at the end of Chapter 1 (p. 23). The five Balance Sheet blocks can be seen:

Fixed assets + Current assets — Current liabilities
           = Shareholders' funds + Long-term loans

There is no particular reason for using M & S's accounts other than that the name is well known, and the layout simple.

Each of these headings in the M & S accounts is now considered, with an explanation in more detail of the

MARKS & SPENCER LTD

BALANCE SHEET AS AT 31 MARCH 1972

	1971			1972	
	£	£		£	£
Fixed assets					
Properties—*Note 5*		154,617,000		167,402,000	
Fixtures and equipment—*Note 6*		13,932,000		14,715,000	
		168,549,000			182,117,000
Net Current Assets					
Stock—at the lower of cost or replacement value		29,642,000		28,397,000	
Debtors and prepayments		5,843,000		5,980,000	
Tax reserve certificates		7,000,000		8,000,000	
Cash and short-term deposits		23,916,000		19,173,000	
		66,401,000			61,550,000

Less:		
Creditors and accrued charges	24,548,000	21,694,000
Corporation tax	20,587,000	21,411,000
Proposed final dividend	15,754,000	17,369,000
	60,889,000	60,474,000
	5,512,000	1,076,000
Net Assets	174,061,000	183,193,000
Debenture Stock—*Note 7*	45,000,000	45,000,000
Preference Shares—*Note 8*	1,350,000	1,350,000
Ordinary Shareholders' Interests—*Note 9*	127,711,000	136,843,000
Capital Employed	174,061,000	183,193,000

J. Edward Sieff
Marcus J. Sieff } *Directors*

F. C. Hirst
J. H. M. Samuel } *Joint Secretaries*

The notes on pages x and x form an integral part of this Balance Sheet.

financial information which companies present to their
shareholders and to the public at large. By the end of this
chapter it is hoped that the reader will be able to read
practically any company's Balance Sheet and understand the
information there available.

Fixed Assets

The first heading on the M & S Balance Sheet is 'fixed assets'.
For M & S these are properties and the fixtures and equipment installed therein. They are the result of the company's
expenditure on items which will allow it to operate its
business — in M & S's case, retail stores.

Fixed assets are a semi-permanent investment in physical
items — the physical assets that the company will use to carry
on its business. These assets will be held for a number of
years, added to and deducted from, as the company carries
on its operations. A fixed asset will not contain items that
the company trades in. For example, with a garage the stock
of cars held for sale to customers will not be treated as a
fixed asset — they will appear in the inventory — but the
breakdown vehicle that the garage uses to collect cars will
appear as a fixed asset, because it is used in the business and
will be held for a number of years. The fixed assets enable
the business to be conducted; they are not bought and sold
for profit.

One of the basic accounting concepts dealt with in Chapter
1 was that of cost valuation. This applies in dealing with the
fixed assets. The original cost of the asset is entered into the
Balance Sheet, and has depreciation set against it. The only
time cost is not used is when the company has revalued its
assets, and then the revaluation figure is used in the Balance
Sheet. In 1964 M & S revalued its properties, so it is the 1964
revaluation figure which is used, and to which is added the
cost of new purchases.

The M & S figures for properties supplied in Note 5 are:

As valued at 31 March 1964	88,457,000
Subsequent additions at cost	71,480,000
	159,937,000
Additions this year (1972)	14,473,000
	174,410,000

Disposals during this year (1972)	776,000
	173,634,000
Accumulated depreciation	6,232,000
Balance Sheet figure	£167,402,000

The company also presents information on the leasehold properties showing that 71% of the properties are freehold and most of the remainder are on leases of over fifty years.

Depreciation
From the above analysis of properties it can be seen that £6,232,000 has been shown as the accumulated depreciation deducted from their value to provide the Balance Sheet figure.

There are several ways of looking at depreciation. Indeed, there have been whole books devoted entirely to this topic. It will be agreed that the wear and tear of the fixed assets must be brought into the company's accounts when deciding the profit generated. If during the year's operations some of the life of the physical assets employed in the business has been used, then this should be taken as a 'cost' in the Profit and Loss Account before declaring a profit. Since the capital of the company should be retained intact, the charging each year of an amount to cover depreciation of the assets of the business in the Profit and Loss Account, to be retained in the business, ensures no reduction in the capital employed. If depreciation were not charged in the accounts, then a false profitability would result.

Before looking at the various methods of allowing for depreciation of fixed assets, it is important properly to grasp the concept. One distinguished academic had an unpleasant experience which highlights some of the problems managers have in understanding depreciation. As a very junior articled clerk he was given the audit of a working mens' club. He balanced the accounts and was sent along to the meeting to present them to the members of the club. He asked if there were any questions on the accounts, and was asked, 'Where's the depreciation gone?' For the layman a very sensible question, but for the trainee accountant it proved very difficult to answer satisfactorily. In the case of M & S Ltd there has been deducted from the Profit and Loss Account

£6,232,000 over the life of the properties, and also in the Balance Sheet £6,232,000 has been deducted from the valuation of those fixed assets. So where has the depreciation gone?

The truthful answer to the question, 'Where's the depreciation gone?', is that we do not know. It has just been used up in the business along with all the other funds that are generated from operations and retained in the company. There is no separate account with £6,232,000 cash in it in the M & S Balance Sheet. The depreciation has been retained in the business, and it is impossible to separate depreciation pounds from retained profit pounds.

However, the mechanical answer is simpler to explain. It is merely a convention, but a realistic one, that causes accountants to show the depreciation as a deduction from the fixed assets in the Balance Sheet. It would be possible to redraft the M & S accounts thus:

Properties at cost or valuation		173,634,000
Fixtures and Equipment	14,715,000	
Net Current Assets	1,076,000	15,791,000
		£189,425,000
Debenture Stock	45,000,000	
Preference Shares	1,350,000	
Ordinary Shareholders' Interest	136,843,000	183,193,000
Accumulated Depreciation		6,232,000
		£189,425,000

In the redrafted Balance Sheet the properties are shown on the assets side, and the accumulated depreciation shown on the liabilities side. The accumulated depreciation is a setting aside of some of the profit to allow for wear and tear on properties, and is retained in the business in just the same way as is retained profit.

There are many ways of calculating depreciation, but the three most common are:

Straight-line method. This is the simplest to operate, and is done by taking the cost of the asset, and dividing it by the anticipated life of the asset.

Reducing-balance method. Under this method a constant percentage of the asset balance is deducted.

Sum-of-the-digits method. This method takes the anticipated life of the asset as the basis for depreciation charges. Thus, if the anticipated life is 10 years, all the digits 1, 2, 3, 4, 5, 6, 7, 8, 9, 10 are added together to give 55. In the first year 10/55ths are charged for the depreciation, in the second year 9/55ths, and so on until the final year has 1/55th charge for depreciation.

The only method that is difficult to calculate is the reducing-balance method, where the correct percentage to apply each year to the balance of the asset value must be sought. There is a formula which assists in this:

$$\text{Depreciation rate} = 1 - \sqrt[n]{\frac{\text{Scrap value}}{\text{Original cost}}}$$

where n = number of years of anticipated life.

However, as with most formulae, there are some problems in its practical application, notably concerning the estimate of scrap value. Most companies which use this method assess a reasonable rate of depreciation and apply that to the assets. In the table below it is assumed that there is a 20% rate used — that is, twice the particular straight-line method rate. The three methods are compared below in the case of a machine which cost £1,000 and has an anticipated life of 10 years.

DEPRECIATION CHARGE

Year	Straight-line	Sum-of-digits	Reducing balance
1	100	182	200
2	100	164	160
3	100	145	128
4	100	127	102
5	100	109	82
6	100	91	66
7	100	73	52
8	100	55	42
9	100	36	34
10	100	18	27
	£1,000	£1,000	£893

It can be seen that under the reducing-balance method there is still £107 of the asset to be written off after ten years; it is not fully depreciated after ten years. Using the reducing-balance method it is impossible to depreciate an asset completely: there will always be some balance left.

The charging of depreciation in the Profit and Loss Account will have an impact of the profit shown each year. If the above table had related to three different firms each of which was making a steady £1,000 profit each year, then each would be showing at the end of the Profit and Loss Account a different 'profit'. Depreciation is an arbitrary assessment by management, but its results are directly seen on the profit retained. It is important to remember this when studying company reports; the depreciation figure should be considered to see if it is reasonable, and if the method is consistent over time. The depreciation charge in M & S accounts for 1971 was £622,600 for properties, and in 1972 £912,000. As a percentage of properties this was 0.4% in 1971 and 0.5% in 1972.

Inflation and Fixed Assets
Under conditions of inflation where the purchasing power of the pound decreases over time, the use of cost as a basis for assessing the investment in fixed assets can be misleading. If, for example, M & S Ltd had purchased all their properties in 1920, and not revalued any of them, to show them in the 1972 Balance Sheet at original cost less accumulated depreciation would mislead as to the real investment, or capital employed in the business.

In January 1973 the Institute of Chartered Accountants produced Exposure Draft 8 which sets out in general terms the recommendations for the treatment of inflation in accounts. But before considering the recommendations for the treatment of inflation, it is worthwhile to consider in more detail the problem itself.

If a lorry driver decided in 1968 to set himself up in business by investing £5,000 in a lorry which he hired out with his services to local builders, and each year after allowing for depreciation — on the straight-line basis of five-year life — he made £1,000 retained profit, what would his Balance Sheet look like in 1973?

Fixed Asset	Cost	Depr.	
Lorry	5,000	5,000	—
Current Asset			
Cash			10,000
			£10,000
Capital			
Initial input		5,000	
Profit		5,000	10,000
			£10,000

The £10,000 appearing in cash is the result of five years' depreciation (at £1,000 per year) plus five years' profit (at £1,000 per year) being retained in the business. These accounts would be signed by the auditor, and the lorry driver would see that his business had doubled in size. However, when he comes to replace his lorry he discovers that it will cost him £10,000 to obtain a new one (the price of lorries having doubled in the last five years). His Balance Sheet upon replacement of the lorry would appear as:

Fixed Asset	Cost	Depr.	
Lorry	10,000	—	10,000
			£10,000
Capital			
Initial input		5,000	
Profit		5,000	10,000
			£10,000

He is now in exactly the same position as he was five years previously. He has a new lorry, and nothing in the bank. So has he really made £5,000 profit? Indeed, if he had been paying tax at 50% of his profits he would have had to borrow money to buy his new lorry.

It is this sort of problem that is at the heart of inflation accounting. It is essential that companies report their real position. The use of historic accounting methods on their own does not allow this when there is inflation on the scale experienced in the U.K. over the last few years.

There are several ways by which the impact of inflation could be brought into companies' accounts:

Replacement cost method. Under this method the replacement cost of the assets would be used as the basis for depreciation.

Current value method. With this method the assets would be valued at their current market value or cost.

With both these methods the drawback is the very great problem of setting the values in the Balance Sheet. For example, what will be the cost of replacing a certain machine? At best it will be a rough guesstimate. It will tend to be too subjective to satisfy either the auditor or the shareholders. A third method is suggested in Exposure Draft 8.

Index method. Using a standard index of the change in the value of the pound, this will be applied to the assets and liabilities of the company to bring them to current pound values.

The choice of index is obviously critical. Whilst every index is open to academic dispute, the Consumer Price Index has been chosen (updated as necessary by the Index of Retail Prices). This index will be applied to the assets and liabilities of a company to bring them to a current purchasing power (CPP) basis. Initially this will require a considerable amount of work by the firm, as all assets have to be brought up into £CPP values, but after this it will be relatively simple.

Companies will produce a Supplementary Current Purchasing Power Statement in their Annual Reports. One of the first companies to do this is Bernard Wardle & Co. Ltd in its 1972 accounts, and it is reproduced here as an illustration of what will be the future pattern of financial reporting.

BERNARD WARDLE & CO. LTD AND SUBSIDIARY COMPANIES

SUPPLEMENTARY CURRENT PURCHASING POWER STATEMENT

	Historical Basis		Current Purchasing Power Basis	
	1971 £'000	1972 £'000	1972 £'000	1971 £'000
Results for the Year				
Sales	6,225	7,504	7,753	6,888

	Historical Basis		Current Purchasing Power Basis	
	1971 £'000	1972 £'000	1972 £'000	1971 £'000
Profits before taxation (Note 2)	399	696	540	290
Taxation	132	252	252	143
Profit after taxation	267	444	288	147
Trading Loss of B. W. F. (Chinley) Ltd after taxation relief	41	—	—	45
	226	444	288	102
Dividends (preference and ordinary)	212	200	200	228
Retained Profits for Year	14	244	88	(126)
Financial Position at end of Year				
Net Current Assets	1,806	1,970	1,970	1,944
Fixed Assets less Depreciation	1,319	1,607	2,014	1,774
	3,125	3,577	3,984	3,718
Less Preference Shares (Note 3)	(200)	(200)	(200)	(215)
Deferred Taxation	(197)	(383)	(383)	(212)
Total Ordinary Shareholders' Interest (Note 4)	2,728	2,994	3,401	3,291
Ratios				
Earnings per Ordinary Share (p)	1.2	2.4	1.6	0.5
Ordinary Dividend Cover (times)	1.1	2.3	1.4	0.4
Return on Ordinary Shareholders' Interest (%)	7.9	14.5	8.2	2.8
Net Assets per Ordinary Share (p)	15.2	16.7	19.0	18.4

Notes
1. The figures in the current purchasing power basis columns were arrived at by converting the corresponding figures in the historical basis columns by reference to changes in the Consumer Price Index between dates of the original transactions and 3rd December, 1972. The current purchasing power basis figures for both 1971 and 1972 are measured in pounds of purchasing power at 3rd December, 1972. The Consumer Price Index at 3rd December, 1972 was taken as 158.9 and at 28th November, 1971 at 147.6 by reference to movements in the Retail Price Index since the Consumer Price Index is only calculated on an annual basis (1963 = 100).

2. *Profit Before Taxation*

The difference between the profit on an historical basis and on a current purchasing power basis is made up as follows:

	1972 £'000	1971 £'000
Profit Before Taxation (historical basis)	696	399
Adjustments to convert to current purchasing power basis: *Stock* Additional charge based on restating cost of stock at the beginning and end of the year in pounds of current purchasing power, thus taking the infla- tionary element out of the profit on the sale of stocks	(64)	(79)
Depreciation Additional depreciation based on cost measured in pounds of current purchasing power, of fixed assets	(64)	(52)
Monetary items Net loss in purchasing power resulting from the effects of inflation on the company's net monetary assets	(48)	(13)
Sales, purchases and all other costs These are increased by the change in the index between the average date at which they occurred and the end of the year. This adjust- ment increases profit as sales exceed the costs in this heading	20	14
	(156)	(130)
Profit Before Taxation (current general purchasing power basis at the end of the year under review)	540	269
Adjustment required to update last year's profit from last year's pounds to this year's pounds		21
Profit Before Taxation (current general purchasing power basis at 3rd December, 1972)	540	290

3. The Preference Share Capital at 28th November, 1971 amounted to £200,000. £200,000 at the beginning of the year is equivalent in purchasing power to £215,000 at 3rd December, 1972. The Company's liability to the Preference Shareholders has been taken as fixed at £200,000 in money terms and, therefore, this liability has declined in real terms from £215,000 to £200,000. This reduction of £15,000 in the Company's obligation in terms of current purchasing power has reduced to £48,000 the net loss of Monetary Items shown in Note 2.

4. Total Ordinary Shareholders' Interest on current purchasing power basis represents

	£
1971	3,291
Retained profit for year	88
Regional Development Grants receivable during year and not released to profit	22
1972	3,401

Auditors' Report on Supplementary Statement

The above supplementary current purchasing power statement has been prepared by the company to restate the results and financial position of the Group by adjusting for the effects of changes in the purchasing power of money. The bases used are indicated in the notes to the statement and are in accordance with those specified in the proposed standard accounting practice (Exposure Draft 8) issued by the Accounting Standards Steering Committee of the accounting profession in the United Kingdom and Ireland on 17th January, 1973. In our opinion the statement is properly computed in accordance with those bases.

Touche Ross & Co.
Chartered Accountants.

Pall Mall Court
67 King Street
Manchester M60 2AT   15th February, 1973.

This book is not the place to go into the details of the mechanical process of inflation accounting, but a simple example will illustrate the method. If a company purchased an asset for £5,000 in year 1 when the Consumer Price Index was 100, and accounts are being prepared for year 2, when the Index has risen to 130, then the CPP value of the asset is:

$$£5,000 \times 130 \div 100 = £6,500$$

If during the year £1,000 has been charged to depreciation, then this becomes:

$$£1,000 \times 130 \div 100 = £1,300$$

The fixed asset section of the Balance Sheet is shown as:

	Historic basis	CPP basis
Fixed Asset	5,000	6,500
less Depreciation	1,000	1,300
	£4,000	£5,200

The results of this approach (but using real index movements) can be seen in Bernard Wardle's accounts, where the fixed assets less depreciation were shown to be £1,607,000 on a historic basis, but £2,014,000 on a CPP basis. The £88,000 profit is a better indication of the profitability of the company than is that shown under the historic accounting basis; dividends and retentions can better be decided in the light of the more accurate protrayal of profit under the CPP basis.

The Supplementary CCP Statement of Bernard Wardle & Co. Ltd is quite straightforward, and gives a good indication of the sort of impact the introduction of inflation accounting will have on companies. It is interesting to see that the tax rate under historical accounting is 36%, but under CPP accounting is 47%.

The Interpretation of Fixed Asset Figures
The M & S Balance Sheet shows a figure of £182,117,000 for the book value of fixed assets. What does this figure convey? Is it

— the market value of the assets if sold?
— the replacement cost of the assets?
— how much the company would be willing to sell the assets for?

The £182,117,000 is none of those values. It merely informs those interested that the assets cost (or have been revalued) a certain amount, and since then have been depreciated by a certain amount, to provide the book value as stated. This is the figure appearing as a balance in the books of the company on 31 March 1972. It is more of an accountants' book-keeping figure than anything else; it is used to ensure that the Balance Sheet balances.

In looking at a Balance Sheet, the date upon which the assets were purchased, or revalued, must be taken into account in the analysis that is done, or the conclusions that are drawn. Until inflation accounting is fully operational this will be a difficult task as, in most Annual Reports, insufficient data are provided to enable this to be done adequately.

Stock
In the 1967 Companies Act it states:

> If the amount carried forward for stock in trade, or work in progress, is material for the appreciation by its members of the company's state of affairs, or of its profit or loss for the financial year, the manner in which that amount has been computed . . . shall be stated by way of note, or in a statement or report annexed, if not otherwise shown. (Schedule 2)

Thus, companies must explain how they have arrived at the value for stock which appears in their Balance Sheet. This requirement is reinforced by the various recommendations of accountancy bodies to their members.

In the case of M & S Ltd the method of valuing stock is shown to have been 'at the lower of cost or replacement value' (£28,397,000). The most common method of valuation is 'the lower of cost and net realisable value'. The Institute of Chartered Accountants in England and Wales publish a *Survey of Published Accounts* which deals with the method of financial reporting of 300 of the larger U.K. companies. In the 1970—71 issue approximately two-thirds of these companies used the 'lower of cost and net realisable value' method of valuing their stock.

The valuation of stock is a very important factor in company reporting, and most professional accountants would agree that it is the most difficult single figure on a Balance Sheet to verify accurately. In the case of a retail organisation such as M & S it is a comparatively easy task. At the year-end the stock of goods in each store can be calculated quite accurately, and this can be added to the value of goods in the pipeline to provide the total stock on hand at 31 March. However, whilst the mechanics are quite easy, the physical size of the task can be gauged from the fact that the company has some 5 million sq. ft of sales space and some 250 stores spread all over the country.

In all companies the stock figure is a valuation, and the end figure for stock in the Balance Sheet depends upon the valuation basis. Stock is important not only for a correct assessment of the capital employed in the business, but also in the calculation of profit in the Profit and Loss Account.

Profit is arrived at by taking the difference between the costs plus expenses, and the revenue for the year. A substantial part of the costs for most companies will be the materials purchased, and used to produce the products that are sold. A simple case could be:

Revenue		£2,000
Opening stock	1,000	
add Purchases	1,000	
	2,000	
less Closing stock	1,000	
Cost of Goods Sold		1,000
Gross Profit		£1,000

If the value of the closing stock is increased by £500 (to £1,500), then the profit for the year becomes £1,500, an equal increase of £500. If the closing stock were to be valued at £500, then the profit would bcome £500. This extreme example illustrates the impact of stock valuation on profitability, and in so doing shows why the valuation of stock is such an important factor in the presentation of information on company performance and financial status.

The auditor is always watchful of inconsistencies in stock valuation, but it is not realistic to expect completely accurate verification of stocks in a large company. He must rely on the company's figures. Auditors make use of statistical sampling methods in verifying stock, and will normally check at least a proportion of the total stock at the company's year-end. A further complication arises from the fact that the auditor is rarely fully competent in the technology of the business he is dealing with, and so is at the mercy of the management of the company during stocktaking exercises.

The stock figure in the Balance Sheet will include:

— raw materials as yet unused
— work-in-progress (part-finished products)
— finished products ready for sale.

The majority of companies provide only a single figure for this composite group, which is not always satisfactory when trying to analyse in detail the financial affairs of that business.

The type of problem which can arise in stock valuation is highlighted in the case of D. F. Bevan (Holdings) Ltd's accounts, where an employee of the company altered the directors' stock figures so that the final evaluations were based partly on fictitious stock levels. The employee was not acting for personal gain, but the accounts prepared on the basis of these stock figures were overstating the real profitability of the company.

Methods of Stock Valuation

A company will know what it has purchased during the year, and how much has been used on the goods sold, but the valuation of closing stock will depend on the cost at which purchased materials have been transferred to production during the year.

If the price of the company's raw material does not alter during the year, then there is no problem in this area. However, most goods fluctuate in price during the year, and so a method of stock valuation must be determined by the company. There are three main methods of stock valuation, and these are illustrated below. There are other methods — for example, standard cost and direct cost — but these will be appreciated after reading Chapters 8 and 9 which deal with these topics.

First in first out (FIFO) method. This method assumes that the oldest items in stock are used first; hence the name. As stock is used, it is charged to production at the earliest price.

Cost of materials purchased:

		£
1,000 lb of metal @ £5 per lb =	5,000	
1,000 lb of metal @ £6 per lb =	6,000	
2,000 lb at a total cost of	£11,000	

less Amount used in production:

1,000 lb @ £5 per lb =	5,000	
500 lb @ £6 per lb =	3,000	
1,500 lb		8,000

Closing Stock: 500 lb @ £6 per lb =   £3,000

Under this method of stock valuation the closing stock of material is close to the replacement cost if prices are rising.

Last in first out (LIFO) method. This method of stock valuation is the reverse of FIFO. Using the same details as above, the stock valuation becomes:

Cost of materials purchased   £11,000

less amount used in production:

1,000 lb @ £6 per lb =	6,000	
500 lb @ £5 per lb =	2,500	8,500

Closing Stock: 500 lb @ £5 per lb =   £2,500

Using LIFO under conditions of rising prices will tend to undervalue the stock on hand, whilst charging in the cost of goods sold a higher amount than under FIFO.

Average cost method. This method uses the average of the price of materials purchased. Using the same figures as previously, the stock valuation becomes:

Cost of materials purchased   £11,000

$$\text{Average cost} = \frac{£11,000}{2,000 \text{ lb}} = £5.5 \text{ per lb}$$

Closing Stock: 500 lb @ £5.5 per lb = £2,750

Comparison of the Three Methods

		FIFO	LIFO	Average
Sales income for Period		£10,000	10,000	10,000
Cost of Goods Sold:				
Opening stock	—		—	—
Purchases	11,000		11,000	11,000
	11,000		11,000	11,000
Closing stock	3,000		2,500	2,750
Cost of goods sold		8,000	8,500	8,250
Gross Profit for Period		£2,000	1,500	1,750

Different methods of stock valuation will create a different profit for the company. But if the company is consistent in its stock valuation method — following one of the basic conventions of accountancy — the long-term difference will be zero. This can be shown:

		FIFO	LIFO	Average
Sales for the Period		£5,000	5,000	5,000
Cost of goods Sold:				
Opening stock	3,000		2,500	2,750
Purchases	—		—	—
	3,000		2,500	2,750
Closing stock	—		—	—
Cost of goods sold		3,000	2,500	2,750
Gross Profit for Period		£2,000	2,500	2,250
Gross Profit for First Period		2,000	1,500	1,750
Gross Profit for Second Period		2,000	2,500	2,250
		£4,000	£4,000	£4,000

Debtors and Prepayments

The next item on the M & S Balance Sheet is that of 'debtors and prepayments' (£5,980,000).

Debtors arise where a company has allowed customers credit facilities. The customer is allowed a certain time before he has to pay for the goods he has received. A typical situation is where a company allows 30 days before it expects customers to pay.

If a company for any reason expects that there may be some of its debtors who will either not pay at all, or only in part, then allowance is made for this in the calculation of year-end debtors. A provision is made for bad or doubtful debts, and deducted from the total debtor figure. The amount appearing in the Balance Sheet can be taken to be debts that the company fully expects to receive in the near future. If there is any unusual movement in bad debts, such as a major customer going into liquidation, then the Annual Report will contain information on this, or otherwise explain why the provision for doubtful debts has been substantially increased.

Clearly, in the case of a retail stores operation there will be very few debtors, all transactions with customers being for cash. Thus, the greater proportion of the £5,890,000 will relate to prepayments.

Prepayments arise when a company pays for a service for some time ahead. For example, rent, rates and insurance are often paid for a year in advance. The amount paid during this year relates to benefits to be received in the following year. Thus, if the Balance Sheet date of a company falls just after the insurance premiums have been paid for the next twelve months, this amount cannot be shown as an expense against the current year's revenue, but must be set aside as a current asset, and termed a prepayment.

Tax Reserve Certificates

M & S held £8,000,000 tax reserve certificates on 31 March 1972. Probably the largest single annual payment a company has to make is the payment of its tax liability to the Inland Revenue. To encourage companies to maintain sufficient liquid resources to meet this requirement, the government

offers tax reserve certificates which can be purchased for cash
and receive tax-free interest when used in paying the tax bill.
These certificates are not transferable and may only be used
in payment of U.K. tax.

Cash and Short-Term Deposits
M & S show £19,173,000 as being held as either cash or on
short-term deposit on 31 March 1972. Short-term deposits
consist of cash that has been lent or deposited for short
periods — even overnight — in return for interest. Most well-
managed companies now make use of the various opportunities open to invest their surplus cash for short periods.
With a business such as M & S where there is a healthy cash
flow from stores there is good sense in short-term lending
which will increase overall profitability. In 1972 the company had an income of £1,277,000 from bank and other
interest receipts.

In the British Home Stores Balance Sheet for 1 April 1972
there was shown £7,750,000 of short-term loans, and the
Royal Dutch/Shell Group showed £109,000,000 invested in
short-term securities in December 1972.

Current Liabilities
M & S show £21,694,000 for creditors and accrued charges in
the Balance Sheet. Creditors are connected with goods or
services delivered to the company which have yet to be paid
for. They are the opposite of debtors.

Accrued charges, or expenses, are the opposite of prepayments. For example, rent may be due at the year-end but has
not yet been paid, as may be electricity and telephone
charges. These expenses must be shown in the Profit and Loss
Account even though they have not yet entered the
company's books, and also appear in the Balance Sheet as
current liabilities.

Corporation Tax
Where taxation appears as a current liability it indicates that
this amount will be paid over to the Inland Revenue within
the next twelve months. For most companies this will be the

tax on the previous year's profits, as there is approximately a
year's lag in incurring the liability and having to pay it over.

Proposed Final Dividend
In the case of M & S the directors have decided to pay a final
dividend of £17,369,000 to shareholders for the year. This
amount cannot be paid out until it has been agreed at the
Annual General Meeting, and so is shown as a current
liability.

The remaining items in the M & S Balance Sheet are
considered later in this book. They are the longer-term
liabilities of the company that will not be paid out for some
time — the Debenture Stock is due to be repaid in
1985/2000 — or not until the company is wound up and the
shareholders receive their initial capital and share of the
reserves back from the realisation of the assets.

2.3. Who Reads the Annual Report?

Having discussed the contents of the Annual Report, and
studied a typical Balance Sheet, the next step is to see who
actually bothers to read a company's Annual Report, and
what sort of things they are looking for. Having done this, it
will be possible to consider how the accounts may be
analysed to answer some of their questions.

Shareholders. They will receive a copy of the Annual Report
which is a statement of the directors' stewardship of
their investment in the company. Many companies now
make use of the Annual Report to illustrate their
products, and in many cases colour photographs
abound. The shareholders, if he reads the report, will
probably be concerned with the growth in revenue and
profit of the company, as well as the dividend the
directors are proposing to pay. However, the majority of
small shareholders do not rely on the Annual Report for
an assessment of the company, but rather on the
analysis done in the financial press.

Potential shareholders. They will be looking at very much
the same information as the existing shareholders, but
again are most likely to rely on professional advice or

newspaper comment for their assessment of the viability of it as an investment.

Investment analysts. These advise investors and, as such, are mainly concerned with the future prospects of the company; it is worthless from the investment point of view to know what profit the company made last year — it is too late to do anything about it. Thus, investment analysts will give only brief time to the historic accounts of the company, and devote most of their effort to an assessment of its potential for growth and profit. This will entail an analysis of the economy and the industry in which the company operates, as well as a detailed assessment of the management of the company. The Annual Report is just the starting-off point for analysis; it is the hors d'oeuvre, not the main course.

Bankers. The banker who allowed overdraft facilities to a company will want to be kept informed as to its operations, and will receive a copy of the Annual Report. The main concern will be whether the money advanced will be repaid as expected. The bank manager is probably the last professional who relies almost completely on the Annual Report for information for decision-making on a company. This state of affairs is changing slowly as bankers become more educated as to what businessmen actually do, and what information is really necessary to monitor company performance.

Customers. A few of the company's customers will be interested in the Annual Report. This is sensible where they are considering placing a large order, and require to know how financially sound the company is; will it still be in business next year to service the product that has been purchased?

Employees. Not many employees spend time studying their company's Annual Report. Today many companies are using their report as a means of communicating with their employees. The whole range of the company's products can be set out, as well as information that employees would not normally see in their work with a single section of the company. The chairman can direct his comments to employees to explain the company's philosophy, or the likely impact of some social change or new piece of legislation.

Whilst the annual 'tribute to staff' can be a mechanical exercise, it can also be used to good effect. In the M & S reports for 1971 and 1972 the chairman actually does explain to staff the board's philosophy towards employees.

Unions. Trade unions are now as competent as most managers in analysing a set of accounts. They will be interested in the growth of the company, and the way in which the profit is being used. It will be interesting to see what impact inflation accounting has on union—management negotiations. Companies will no longer be overstating their real profitability.

Creditors. These will be looking at the company to see if it is creditworthy, and whether they will receive payment. Their main concern will be with the solvency or liquidity of the company.

Management. As has already been mentioned, the Annual Report can be used as an effective communication tool by the directors, and the managers in the company will probably give some attention to what is said there. They will also be able to see how their bit of the company's operations fits into the overall picture.

The directors will certainly study the Annual Report, and two of them sign it. But they will be mainly concerned with its preparation, and trying to assess how it will be received by those people who will read, analyse and comment on it. They will not be trying to run the company on the basis of the Annual Report. Any board of directors that has to wait until the annual accounts are prepared to discover if they made a profit or a loss during the year can hardly be said to be in control of the company.

2.4. The Analysis of Published Accounts

There used to be a bank manager who was well known for his financial abilities. When a customer brought in a set of accounts he would study the Profit and Loss Account and the Balance Sheet for less than one minute before taking the decision of how much money to advance. His record was quite good, and his reputation as a financial wizard tremendous. It was only when he retired that he passed his secret on to his colleagues. If the customer had blue eyes he gave him everything he asked for, if they were brown he gave 50% of what was requested, and any other colour received nothing.

That the really professional finance man or accountant can pick up a set of accounts and in a matter of seconds take major long-term decisions is a myth. It requires a lot of work, as well as experience, to make a sensible analysis of a company's accounts, and it is to this task that the remainder of this chapter and Chapter 3 are devoted.

In any analysis one must first decide what it is that is being looked for. The way in which the main categories of people will be looking at the accounts, and the sort of questions they will be asking, has already been mentioned; there follows a series of ratios which can be used to assist them.

Probably the most common question concerning a company's affairs is whether or not it will be able to pay its bills and stay in business. This will not only concern those external to the firm — the creditors and the bank manager — but also the management of the company who wish to ensure the continued survival of their company, and their jobs.

Measures of Solvency and Liquidity

In Chapter 1 the ability of a company to show a healthy profit in its accounts, and to go bankrupt in the following month, was mentioned. Just because a company is profitable does not mean it has any cash resources available. It is arguable that the control and management of liquid resources in a company is more important than the generation of profit. A company can make a loss and have plenty of time to do something about it — there are several major companies who have suffered such a situation of several years' losses or very low profits — but any company which finds itself short of cash is in a much more critical situation, and a liquidation is the likely outcome. Put in simple terms:

No cash = No business
No profit = Challenge to management

In assessing a company's ability to meet short-term liabilities — to pay its current liabilities as they fall due — the relationship between current assets and current liabilities is vital. To illustrate this, consider the five companies' working capital information given below (£m, 1971 figures):

	Mitchell	Laing	Costain	M & S	BHS
Current liabilities	14.4	17.9	25.8	60.9	11.6
Current assets	17.4	30.5	31.6	66.4	19.2
Working capital	3.0	12.6	5.8	5.5	7.6

There are two main ratios which are employed to assess a company's short-term financial viability. The first of these is the current ratio, which is calculated:

$$\frac{\text{Current assets}}{\text{Current liabilities}}$$

This, when expressed as a ratio, describes the working capital situation of the company, and for the five companies is:

Mitchell	Laing	Costain	M & S	BHS
1.2:1	1.7:1	1.2:1	1.1:1	1.6:1

All these companies have at least a 1:1 current ratio. That is, they have more current assets than current liabilities. This knowledge is useful in that it shows that if the company were forced to pay out all its currect liabilities there would be sufficient funds in current assets to do so.

Any company which pays out its current liabilities will follow a series of steps:

1. Write cheques to the value of its cash holding.
2. Call in cash from customers.
3. Sell the inventory on the best terms possible.
4. Sell some of the fixed assets.

Normally only the first two steps will be necessary. Any company which reaches the step of selling off fixed assets to pay current liabilities is almost past redemption. Current liabilities can be expected to be paid from Current assets. A company that has a current ratio of more than 1:1 is at least technically solvent.

There are no standards for the current ratio; what is safe and acceptable will depend on many factors — size, industry, timing of the Balance Sheet, etc. But it is generally accepted that companies should show a current ratio of greater than 1:1, and preferably nearer 2:1. There are often exceptions; for example, Pontin's Ltd — the holiday firm — whose working capital data (in £m) were:

	30 April 1971	*1972*
Current Liabilities	5.3	6.8
Current Assets	1.3	1.4
Negative Working Capital	£4.0	£5.4

is a healthy trading company, but owing to the timing of its year-end shows an unusually adverse working capital position. Had the Balance Sheet been taken out at a different time of the year, the working capital situation would have been completely different.

In dealing with the valuation of stock earlier in this chapter, some of the problems and difficulties associated with it were mentioned. If a really strict appraisal of a company's solvency is required, it is best to leave stock out of the current assets, and to take only the liquid assets into consideration. If a company were forced into the position of having to realise its stock quickly, it is doubtful if it would even recover their cost value, so it is realistic to ignore this item for this purpose. The ratio then becomes

$$\frac{\text{Current assets} - \text{Stock}}{\text{Current liabilities}}$$

and for the five companies the ratio is

Mitchell	*Laing*	*Costain*	*M & S*	*BHS*
0.3:1	1:1	0.9:1	0.6:1	0.9:1

Mitchell appears the weakest under this ratio — sometimes termed the 'acid test'. What does this mean? It means that if the company were forced to pay out its current liabilities quickly, and the investment in stocks and works-in-progress was not capable of being turned into cash in time, then the company would be incapable of paying in full without recourse to borrowing.

The ideal ratio should be at least 1:1, but, again, there are no standards and all the various factors must be considered in assessing a company's acceptability under this ratio. There is a danger in having too good a ratio here, in that the company becomes an attractive proposition to other companies who could release the liquid assets into their own operations. Too high a ratio could also indicate that the company is not making adequate use of its finances; cash by itself does not generate much profit for a company — unless of course it is a financial institution.

There is one final ratio that can usefully be employed in this area of analysis. This is the current liquidity ratio:

$$\frac{\text{Current liabilities} - (\text{Current assets} - \text{Stock})}{\text{Profit before tax and interest}} \times 365$$

For the five companies this ratio is:

	Mitchell	Laing	Costain	M & S	BHS
Number of days	2,864	−37	235	176	51

Mitchell again appears the weakest. This ratio shows that it would take Mitchell 2,864 days (almost eight years), working at normal profit levels experienced in 1971, to pay off the deficit between current liabilities and liquid assets. Laing is so liquid that it has a negative figure for 1971.

These ratios are merely indicators of the company's solvency and liquidity, and do not in themselves predict insolvency or cash problems. They can act as warnings that a company is in a precarious situation. Mitchell went into liquidation in January 1973, but had been operating very successfully in previous years on similar ratios. All that could be said based on these ratios was that if anything happened to slow down the flow of funds into the company there was very little cushion there to assist survival.

The importance of relating the ratio to the particular firm being dealt with cannot be stressed too much. If a comparison of the above five firms with their 1971 figures is to be made, then little is to be gained from comparing Costain with BHS — who happen to have the same 0.9:1 acid test ratio. It is more realistic and useful to compare BHS with M & S as they are in the same business, and it can be seen that in all the ratios used so far BHS is more liquid than M & S. The companies have a different approach to financial management.

To allow a more meaningful comparison of BHS and M & S, the Tesco Stores figures are used. One way of measuring the use being made of cash in the business is to look at the velocity of its movement. This can be measured using the ratio of:

$$\frac{\text{Sales}}{\text{Average cash balance}}$$

Another ratio which can be used in this area is:

$$\frac{\text{Cash}}{\text{Current assets}} \times 100$$

which shows what proportion of the current assets is held in cash or short-term deposits. These ratios, based on the 1972 Balance Sheets of the three companies, are:

	M & S	BHS	Tesco
Cash as a percentage of current assets	31.3%	44.9%	5.0%
Cash velocity	21.5	9.2	166.5

The amount of cash that Tesco holds compared with the other two retail organisations can be seen to account for the very rapid cash movement through the company. BHS can be seen to hold a lot more cash than either of the other two.

The year-ends of these three companies all fall around March and so it is possible to make a meaningful comparison of their figures. Had one of them had a year-end in

December, then comparison would have been less realistic, because of the entirely different trading conditions that retail companies experience at that time compared with the rest of the year.

Profitability Measures

Most people looking at the Annual Report of a company will be concerned with an assessment of its profitability. The most common ratio used for this measurement is the return on capital employed (ROCE):

$$\text{ROCE} = \frac{\text{Profit}}{\text{Capital employed}} \times 100$$

As this is the most commonly used ratio, it also tends to be the most commonly misused ratio. Before it is possible to compare ROCEs it is essential that all the terms in the calculation are clearly defined. What sort of profit is being used? Pre-tax, post-tax, before interest, after depreciation, or what? And how is the capital employed calculated: total assets, net assets, or some other basis? As far as this book is concerned, the definition of 'capital employed' is:

Fixed assets + Current assets − Current liabilities

Using the three retail companies for 1972, their ROCE was:

	M & S	BHS	Tesco
Using pre-tax profit	29%	27%	34%
Using post-tax profit	19%	15%	20%

This ratio measures the efficiency of management in generating profit on the capital employed in the company. There are problems with its application in that the fixed assets are taken at the Balance Sheet valuation. Ideally, all the assets in the companies should be valued in the same manner. Also a company may not own many fixed assets, because it rents or leases them. This can distort the comparison in some cases.

It is possible to compare the ROCE from retailing with that of another industry, and so ICI 1972 figures can be taken:

Pre-tax ROCE	7.5%
Post-tax ROCE	5.8%

As would be expected, the return of ICI is different — much lower — than that of retailing organisations. But what accounts for the difference? Partly it is due to the fact that retail companies do not have to have the vast manufacturing investment required in ICI, and partly to the fact that profit levels are different. This can be illustrated by looking at the relationship of sales income to the other factors involved.

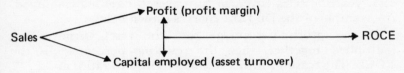

An example of the Du Pont chart

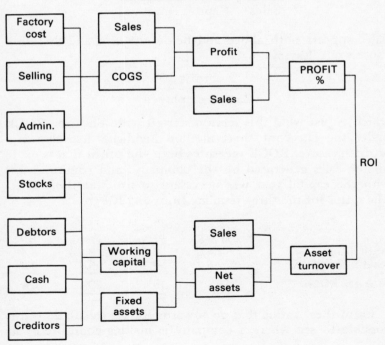

Sales are used to generate profit — the mark-up or profit margin on sales — and use the capital employed in the business, which can be measured in the asset turnover ratio: how many times each year the assets are turned over by the sales generated by their use. Many companies are now making use of an extension of this concept in the use of the Du Pont chart (named after the company which pioneered work in this area in the 1950s). This chart takes the Profit and Loss Account of the company and expresses it in the single ratio of profit to sales. The Balance Sheet of the company is also reduced to a single ratio, in this case the number of times each year the sales cover, or turn over, the capital employed. An example of the Du Pont chart is shown below:

If the profit percentage and the asset turnover are multiplied together, then the resulting percentage is the ROCE. The reason for this is simple. The two ratios are:

$$\frac{\text{Profit}}{\text{Sales}} \times \frac{\text{Sales}}{\text{Capital employed}}$$

Sales appears both above and below the line, and therefore cancels out, leaving:

$$\frac{\text{Profit}}{\text{Capital employed}}$$

which is just what this section started with. Showing ROCE under the Du Pont chart method highlights its value as a profit measure. ROCE measures both the profit that is made on the sales generated by the company, and combines this with the capital that was necessary to produce those sales. The ratios for the three retailing firms and ICI are:

	M & S	BHS	Tesco	ICI
Profit margin	7.4%	6.6%	3.2%	6.4%
Asset turnover	2.5	2.3	6.1	0.9
After-tax ROCE	19%	15%	20%	6%

From these ratios that go towards ROCE calculations it is possible to see where a company is making good use of its resources, as well as whether the profit margin on sales is satisfactory. Tesco, working on very small margins, produce their good ROCE through a very high sales volume on the capital employed in the business. And it is the high capital employed that causes ICI to have such a poor showing — it is not turning over its capital employed during the year.

ROCE and Revaluation

As ROCE is a well-known and well-used ratio for assessing company performance, it is one to which management give attention. If a company were to revalue the assets of the company this would cause an automatic reduction in the ROCE percentage, and this is one of the reasons why companies do not always favour an asset revaluation.

Indeed, it can be argued that a board of directors should only revalue the company's assets on two occasions: firstly, where a takeover is threatened, so that the purchasing company can at least be made to pay the best price possible for the assets; and secondly, where the company wishes to borrow more money on the strength of the assets shown in the Balance Sheet. To revalue at any other time will show an adverse picture of the directors' activities.

Other Working Capital Measures

There are several other important ratios which can be used to assess the performance and financial management of a company. Stock is part of the capital employed in the business. The company has used some of its funds to build up stock. If the company holds too much stock it will be wasting its financial resources by locking them up in an unused asset. If the company holds too little stock it will lose sales revenue and profit through not being able to service its customers. To measure how much is tied up in stock and also how quickly the stock is turned over, there are two ratios that can be used:

$$\frac{\text{Stock}}{\text{Current assets}} \quad \text{and} \quad \frac{\text{Sales}}{\text{Stock}}$$

The first of these shows what proportion of the current assets is held in stock, and the second shows how many times during the year the stock is turned over by the sales. For the four companies these ratios are:

	M & S	BHS	Tesco	ICI
Stock as a percentage of current assets	46%	48%	87%	37%
Stock turnover	16	9	11	5

The two that stand out here are Tesco with a very high proportion of their current assets being held in stock, and ICI with a very low stock turnover. The greater the stock turnover figure, the better for the company. If the goods are being sold at a profit, then the more that are sold the better the profit at the year-end.

Having sold the goods to a customer, there is then normally a delay before payment is received. This is the credit period, and can be used to assess how well management is speeding the flow of cash through the business. The ratio is calculated as:

$$\frac{\text{Debtors}}{\text{Average daily sales}}$$

For ICI the figure is 90 days for 1972 compared with 88 days in 1971. This means that on average ICI is allowing three months' credit to customers. There are problems with this ratio in that it must be assumed that the situation shown at the Balance Sheet date is representative of that holding for the rest of the year.

Debtors can also be used to assess the overall soundness of the company's short-term financial situation when they are compared with creditors in the ratio:

$$\frac{\text{Debtors}}{\text{Creditors}}$$

If there is a trend observed in a company where the creditors begin to outweigh the debtors, this can be a sign of over-trading. The company is stretching itself too far. Cash is called in as quickly as possible from debtors, and creditors are made to wait as long as possible before payment.

2.5. Real-Life Accounts

It is now recommended that the reader obtain a set of published accounts for any company he knows, and see if he can understand them. This is the best possible test of this chapter's efficacy. But there will be several bits of terminology in real-life accounts which have not so far been considered. A short list of the most common terminology is given below to assist the full understanding of any company's Annual Report.

Group or Consolidated Accounts

Most of the public companies are groups, that is, more than one company trading together. ICI in 1972 had 426 subsidiary companies. The Companies Acts require that the shareholders shall have full information on the group's activities, and so in the Annual Report of a group of companies the following accounts will appear:

— Group Profit and Loss Account (Consolidated)
— Group Balance Sheet (Consolidated)
— main company Balance Sheet

Where a group of companies is being studied there will be two Balance Sheets: the main one listing the total assets and liabilities of all companies in the group, and the other showing the financial standing of the parent or main company. The Group or Consolidated Profit and Loss Account shows the whole trading activities of the companies in the group.

'Consolidated' means that the whole organisation has been brought together. All the sales made by the various companies are added together, as are all the costs to provide the Profit and Loss Account. The Balance Sheet is the total of all the assets and liabilities of all companies in the group.

In studying a set of consolidated accounts it is suggested that the parent or main company Balance Sheet be ignored.

Goodwill

One of the first concepts considered in this book, the monetary quantification concept, specified that if an item could not be quantified in monetary terms, then it could not be brought into the books of account. So where 'goodwill' appears in a Balance Sheet it means something different from the normal usage of that word.

Goodwill can only arise where a company has been purchased by another company for more than the book value of its assets. It is a figure which includes the normal 'goodwill' of a business but will also cover all the other items which do not appear in an accounting Balance Sheet:

- management
- know-how
- trade names
- patents

To make the books balance, the accountant must take the difference between what was paid for the company, and what the Balance Sheet of that company shows, as goodwill, and show it on the asset side of the Group Balance Sheet.

Minority Interest
It sometimes happens that one of the subsidiaries is not completely owned by the parent company. There are some shareholders other than the parent company. To show the shareholders what really belongs to them in the group accounts, it is necessary to show separately the amount that belongs to shareholders outside the group — the minority or outsider shareholders.

Share Premium Account
This arises where a company issue shares at a price greater than their nominal value — they are issued at a premium. As the only amount of share capital shown in the Balance Sheet is the nominal value of the shares, the additional amount raised must be shown separately in the Share Premium Account. It is not possible, in the U.K., to issue shares at a discount and thereby create the opposite type of account.

Tax Equalisation Reserve Account
Sometimes the amount of depreciation of assets allowed by the government changes, and so the asset value is different

from that shown by the directors of the company in their own books. If the company were to show in its Profit and Loss Account the full amount of tax allowances which it has taken, then the profit in that year would be very high — if the allowances were substantially greater than those normally taken. In the following year there would be few allowances available, since they would all have been taken in the previous year, and so profits would be low.

Companies could be showing fluctuating profits in the Profit and Loss Account merely because of tax allowances. To overcome this, companies create a reserve into which they place and withdraw to enable them to show a steadier profitability to shareholders. This is often termed a Tax Equalisation Reserve Account.

Deferred Taxation
This heading is sometimes used to describe corporation tax which is not payable for at least 12 months after the Balance Sheet date, but is also now used more commonly to describe the reserve detailed in Tax Equalisation Reserve Account above.

3 Financial Planning

Chapter 2 examined some of the basic ratios which can be used in the analysis of published accounts. These ratios can be used by people outside the company, who have no access to detailed internal accounting data, to answer such questions as: can the company pay its debts? what is the company's profitability and growth record? and so on. However, as the ratios so far discussed rely entirely on publicly available information, they are inevitably limited. In order really to understand and interpret a company's performance one must go behind the Annual Report and obtain more information for analysis and comparison. The Annual Report, by itself, does not provide sufficient information for a really acceptable analysis.

For example, in the 1972 Annual Report of Marks & Spencer Ltd it is possible to extract further information than that contained in the Profit and Loss Account, which shows the £53,766,000 profit for the year (see p. 25), by reading the notes, the Directors' Report and the Chairman's Statement:

Income:

Turnover for the year:		
	Sales of clothing in the U.K.	326,809,000
	Sales of foods in the U.K.	126,651,000
	Export sales	9,562,000
		£463,022,000
	Interest received	£1,277,000

Expenses:

Repairs and maintenance	2,767,000
Depreciation	4,620,000
Contributions to pension scheme and Benevolent Fund	1,242,000
Directors' emoluments	398,000

Auditors' remuneration	18,000
Debenture interest	3,178,000
Charitable donations	211,000
Aggregate remuneration of employees	31,088,000
The cost of price reduction due to taxation changes	1,270,000

These figures, together with the Profit and Loss Account and Balance Sheet information, are almost all that can be found in the report to assist in an assessment of the company's performance in 1972. The company has met fully the requirements of the 1948 and 1967 Companies Acts, and presented clearly and simply the details of its operations. The accounts of any other company will show the same sort of information – a general, not a detailed, outline of the previous year's operations.

Whilst these figures are of some interest when compared either with previous years or with those of the competition, they do not allow a full understanding of the profitability of the company. It is impossible to discover the comparative profitability of food sales against clothing sales or to answer any of the really important questions as to how M & S managed to make such a good, and continued, profit.

It is possible to use some of the data to draw comparisons between the three retailing firms used in Chapter 2 (based on 1972 accounts, in £000):

	M & S	BHS	Tesco
Profit per employee	1.5	0.6	0.5
Sales per employee	13	6	9
Average sales per store	1,867	873	380
Average profit per store	217	100	21
Average wage bill per store	125	97	30

An analysis such as this would enable a useful discussion to be held as to the comparative success of the management of these companies, but several other factors would have to be taken into account – for example, Tesco has the largest number of stores, but they tend to be smaller than those of M & S and BHS – for a proper understanding of performance.

A manager working in a company will have access to full

information on all aspects of operations, and in his work he will make use of this information to analyse past and forecast future results. Before the use of ratios as predictors is considered, one final tool for the analysis of published accounts must be mentioned — funds flow analysis — which will also be used in financial forecasting.

3.1. Funds Flow Analysis
The annual Balance Sheet of a company describes the assets and liabilities of the company at the year-end. The operations of the company will have resulted, during that year, in a continual flow of funds; the assets and liabilities of the company will be changing throughout the year, particularly in the area of working capital. The terms 'funds' is used in preference to 'cash' because many of the changes will not be in strict cash terms, but relate to items such as debtors and creditors which are not necessarily at the time of analysis cash items. The profit that is shown in the Profit and Loss Account, and which will normally be one of the main sources of funds to a company, is, as was discussed in Chapter 1, not a 'cash' profit, following the accrual concept.

The movements in the assets and liabilities of a company can be analysed into a Funds Flow Statement by comparing two consecutive Balance Sheets. For Marks and Spencer Ltd, using the 1972 Balance Sheet on p. 30, the main blocks are (in £'000):

	1971	*1972*	*Increase*	*Decrease*
Fixed Assets	168,549	182,117	13,568	
Current Assets	66,401	61,550		4,851
Current Liabilities	60,889	60,474		415
Debenture Stock	45,000	45,000		
Preference Shares	1,350	1,350		
Ordinary Shareholders' Interest	127,711	136,843	9,132	

If the 1971 figures are deducted from the 1972 figures the increase or decrease can be shown. This is the change that has occurred between the two Balance Sheets, which has taken place over the twelve month time period covered by the Profit and Loss Account.

In completing the funds flow analysis, one question has to be asked for each of the changes that have occurred: is it a source or a use of funds? Or, to put the question another way, has the change resulted from a use of 'cash' or from the receipt of 'cash'? Cash is placed in inverted commas because, as has already been mentioned, the Balance Sheet items are not necessarily reflected in real cash, but may be the right to receive cash in the future, or the obligation to pay it out in the future.

So for each item that has changed, this question can be answered. The increase in fixed assets of £13,568,000 is a use of the funds available to the company. It has increased the total investment in fixed assets by this amount. The decrease of £4,851,000 in current assets is a source of funds to the company. The company has released from current assets this amount; the tying-up of funds in this area has been reduced. The decrease of £415,000 in current liabilities is a use of funds. The company has reduced its liabilities, and to do this will have had to use some of the available funds. The increase in the shareholders' interest of £9,132,000 is a source of funds to the company. A liability on the company has increased which means there has been made available for use some more funds. For example, the retained profit of the company will have been included here, and this is clearly a source of funds.

These changes can be shown (in £ 000) as:

Sources of Funds:
Decrease in current assets	4,851	
Increase in shareholders' interest	9,132	£13,983

Uses of Funds:
Increase in fixed assets	13,568	
Decrease in current liabilities	415	£13,983

If the original Balance Sheets used in the analysis balanced, and the subtractions have been done accurately, then the Funds Flow Statement must also balance. The sources of funds must exactly equal the uses of funds if the rules of book-keeping are maintained.

This analysis for M & S is clearly inadequate, but before it is explained how a more detailed and realistic Funds Flow Statement could be prepared, it is necessary to see why it is worth the effort.

The main use that is made of the Balance Sheet of a company when assessing its financial state is to use the series of ratios discussed in Chapter 2, and to see how these compare with previous years. Is there a trend developing? And if so, what does it indicate? What is being looked at is the changes that have occurred over time. Funds flow analysis looks at those changes. Anything that has not moved since the previous Balance Sheet is ignored; it is the changes that are highlighted. Funds flow analysis pre-digests the Balance Sheet; it tells what has changed. Where have the financial resources of the company been generated, and how have they been used? If a Funds Flow Statement is prepared for a company for five years, then it provides the opportunity to assess the financial management of that company much more easily than if five years' Balance Sheets were studied.

Detailed Funds Flow Analysis
To appreciate fully what has been happening to the financial situation of a company, one must consider each item on the Balance Sheet in some detail. The Funds Flow Statement provided above for Marks & Spencer Ltd is not detailed enough. To assist the preparation of a full Funds Flow Statement there are some simple rules which can be employed. These are:

Increases in assets are uses of funds.
Decreases in assets are sources of funds.

Increases in liabilities are sources of funds.
Decreases in liabilities are uses of funds.

Armed with these simple rules, it is possible to prepare a funds flow analysis for any company using the published accounts.

It is also possible to relate the change in the cash position of the company between the two Balance Sheets to the actual flow of funds. Where this is done, the four rules given above need to have 'funds' replaced by 'cash', and for M & S for the year ended 31 March 1972 the explanation of the £4,743,000 reduction in cash and short-term deposits is:

CASH MOVEMENT, 1972

		£'000
Opening cash and short-term deposits balance		23,916
Add:		
Decrease in stock	1,245	
Increase in corporation tax	824	
Increase in dividend	1,615	
Disposal of properties	776	
Increase in retained profit	9,132	
Depreciation of properties	912	
Depreciation of fixtures and equipment	3,575	18,079
		41,995
Less:		
Increase in debtors	137	
Increase in tax certificates	1,000	
Increase in properties	14,473	
Increase in fixtures and equipment	4,358	
Decrease in creditors	2,854	22,822
Closing cash and short-term deposits balance		£19,173

If the Funds Flow Statement covers several years it illustrates the sources of funds the management of the company have available. Where is the company obtaining its finance? How much is from internally generated sources — retained profit and depreciation, the cash flow of the firm? And how much is coming from increases in short-term liabilities — not paying creditors on time, or increasing overdraft facilities? How much from the raising of long-term loans or fresh issues of capital? And how is the amount available being used by the company? How much is being put into fixed assets, or invested in increased stockholding or credit to customers? The Funds Flow Statement provides the key to understanding the financial policy of the company's management. It tells one where management is obtaining finance, and how it is being used.

Combined with ratio analysis of the type described in Chapter 2, funds flow analysis gives the maximum information that can be extracted from a company's Annual

Report. Anything else requires a more detailed knowledge of the company's internal information system. It is towards this that the remainder of this chapter looks, with particular attention to how ratio analysis and funds flow analysis can be used in forward planning.

3.2. Ratios as Predictors

Ratios are often used solely to inform about past experience or the current situation of a firm. But the same ratios that are used for this purpose can be used to assess the implications, in financial terms, of management's policies. For example, it is not unusual for a company to take a longer-term decision without fully assessing its financial impact. The company below has a turnover of £1,200,000 per year, and depreciates its fixed assets on a straight-line basis of £50,000 per year.

BALANCE SHEET, 31 DECEMBER — I

Shareholders' Interest	400,000	Fixed Assets		200,000
Current Liabilities	200,000	Current Assets:		
		Stock	200,000	
		Debtors	100,000	
		Cash	100,000	400,000
	£600,000			£600,000

The company decides that it is possible to double the turnover in the coming year and to produce profits of £100,000. This plan is met with enthusiasm and carried out. The following year shows the Balance Sheet as:

BALANCE SHEET, 31 DECEMBER — II

Shareholders' Interest	500,000	Fixed Assets		150,000
Current Liabilities	400,000	Current Assets:		
		Stock	350,000	
		Debtors	400,000	
		Cash	—	750,000
	£900,000			£900,000

The company has achieved its plan but, in so doing, has run into financial problems. Ratio analysis can show that the current ratio has moved from 2:1 to 1.9:1, and the 'acid test' remained constant at 1:1, but the company has no cash with which to carry on its operations.

A series of simple calculations as outlined below could have shown this possibility to the company's management before the plan was put into operation.

Financing Debtors and Stock
The company was allowing approximately 30 days' credit — this explains how one month's sales appear as debtors in the first year's Balance Sheet. Had management been asked what credit they would have to extend to double sales, they might have been able to predict that it would be 60 days. From this information it would be possible to predict what the debtors figure would be in next year's Balance Sheet:

$$\frac{60}{365} = \text{one-sixth of predicted sales of £2,400,000}$$

$$= £400,000$$

Ignoring all else for the moment, management could have asked the question: how is this £300,000 increase in debtors to be financed? Can the company afford it?

To answer that question, the concept of funds flow analysis illustrated earlier in this chapter can be used. What are the sources of funds going to be during the next year for the company?

Profit	£100,000	
Depreciation	50,000	
	150,000	
Cash	100,000	£250,000

Even if the £100,000 cash balance is used, there will only be £250,000 available, and this is insufficient to meet the £300,000 extra debtors. The company must therefore either slow down on the payment of creditors, obtain overdraft facilities from the bank, or obtain longer-term loans. At the beginning of the year, whilst management is still considering its plans, it would be possible to show that the increase likely in debtors would stretch the company's finances considerably.

If the change in stock was also considered, then the likely year-end financial picture becomes clear. The company is turning its stock over approximately once every two months; the stock turnover to sales is six times per year. If the company's management had been asked at the beginning of the year what the likely impact on stock would be of the doubling of turnover, they might have been able to show that stockholding would not have to double with sales, and they should achieve a stock turnover of approximately seven times per year. Such a stock turnover would have shown that at the year-end there would be £343,000 stock — this being one-seventh of £2,400,000.

Thus, if the increase in stock of £143,000 is added to the increase in debtors of £300,000, it can be seen that the company must find finance for an additional £443,000 to put its plan of doubling sales revenue into operation. To do this would require running down the cash resources to an unacceptable level, and increasing the short-term borrowing from creditors, perhaps to the detriment of future relations.

Had this knowledge been available to the company it could have planned either to alter the increase in sales, or to borrow funds well in advance of any crisis.

Creditors

In just the same way that calculations have been done for debtors they can be carried out for creditors. But here it is better if the level of creditors is related to the purchases that are made. If, in the example given above, purchases of materials had accounted for £800,000 in the first year, and the whole £200,000 current liabilities represented materials creditors, then the length of credit can be seen to be:

$$365 \div \left(\frac{£800,000}{£200,000} \right) = 91 \text{ days}$$

If the company was expecting to maintain these relationships with the increased sales, then if 91 days' credit is taken on the £1,600,000 materials purchases the figure for current liabilities in the next year's Balance Sheet would be:

$$\frac{91}{365} = \frac{1}{4} \times £1,600,000$$

$$= £400,000$$

Using these simple ratios it is possible to draft a pro-forma Balance Sheet which can then assist management to assess the viability of their plans in financial terms.

If the company thought it possible to increase the credit taken from suppliers to 120 days, then it would be able to show in the next year's Balance Sheet:

$$\frac{120}{365} = \frac{1}{3} \times £1,600,000$$

$$= £533,000$$

This additional £133,000 (£533,000 − £400,000 current liabilities) could be used to finance the increase in stock and debtors required under the doubling of turnover plan. The Balance Sheet at the end of the next year would then have appeared as follows:

BALANCE SHEET, 31 DECEMBER — III

Shareholders' Interest	500,000	Fixed Assets		150,000
Current Liabilities	530,000	Current Assets:		
		Stock	350,000	
		Debtors	400,000	
		Cash	130,000	880,000
	£1,030,000			£1,030,000

A Funds Flow Statement would show what has occurred since the first Balance Sheet:

Sources		Uses	
Retained profit	100,000	Increase in stock	150,000
Depreciation	50,000	Increase in debtors	300,000
Increase in current liabilities	330,000	Increase in cash	30,000
	£480,000		£480,000

This sort of analysis, in which ratios are used to predict future figures rather than interpret historic ones, is commonly undertaken in most financially aware companies when assessing plans and investment programmes. The historic experience can be used to give the ratios viability, and the figures that are produced can be of great assistance to management in looking at the vital factor, the impact of their plans on the financial state of their company.

3.3. The Operating Cycle

A further, and more detailed way in which management can analyse their operations with the assistance of ratios is to be found in the operating cycle. This measures the time taken from the initial input of funds into raw materials to commence the cycle to the final receipt of funds from customers after the goods have been sold. The operating cycle not only provides a useful tool for management but also illustrates the way in which a series of ratios can be combined to provide useful information.

THE OPERATING CYCLE

Days

Raw materials turnover $= \dfrac{\text{Average raw materials stock}}{\text{Average daily materials purchases}} =$

less

Credit taken on materials $= \dfrac{\text{Average creditors}}{\text{Average daily materials purchases}} =$

add

Production time $= \dfrac{\text{Average work-in-progress}}{\text{Average daily cost of goods sold}} =$

Finished goods turnover $= \dfrac{\text{Average finished stock}}{\text{Average daily cost of goods sold}} =$

Credit allowed $= \dfrac{\text{Average debtors}}{\text{Average daily sales}} =$

Time (in days) of operating cycle $=$

Each ratio in the operating cycle measures one aspect of the firm's work. The raw materials turnover tells how long the company's funds are employed in this area. The average stock is found by taking the opening and closing stocks and dividing by two; the average daily purchases by taking the total of purchases for the year and dividing by 365. From this is deducted the average length of credit taken by the firm to show the net time funds are employed in raw materials. The operating cycle then follows through into production and eventual finished stock with similar calculations. The final ratio is that of the credit period allowed by the firm to customers.

The shorter the operating cycle, the better for the firm in that it will be making the best use of available funds by a short cycle. A company doing the calculations for the cycle can quickly see where the bottlenecks in their operations are. Which point in the cycle is the slowest, and why? The ratios in the operating cycle do not answer any questions. They merely indicate that questions should be asked of certain areas of the firm's operations.

3.4. Financial Planning

The chairman of a small manufacturing company when asked about planning said, 'We haven't time for plans; we just make a profit.' Unfortunately this is by no means unusual for smaller companies; planning is often seen as a waste of effort. By the time the plans are completed, many of the factors and assumptions will have changed, making the plans less useful. However, every company should have some planning activity taking place, otherwise it is likely to drift from crisis to crisis with no sense of purpose or direction.

The first step in the financial planning exercise is for the management of the company to decide where it is they wish the company to go. What are they in business for? This is not necessarily a financial question, but the answer to it will have to be translated into financial terms to assess its viability and impact on the company and its future. Management should ask several questions as to the overall direction of the company in the future:

What is the company's business?
What are the key factors that will affect this in the future?
What are the company's strengths?
What are the company's weaknesses?
What are the limiting factors on future growth?

The discussion that should be stimulated by each of these questions will cover not only the internal factors having a bearing on the company's future, but also the many external factors:

— government changes, legislation, taxation, etc.
— changes in social tastes and behaviour
— economic changes
— technological changes.

Management will have to make assumptions as to how these factors will change in the future, and what their impact will be on the company's growth potential. A successful attempt at this sort of analysis should include a written outline of each director's assessment of internal and external factors affecting the company's future. If each director writes down the assumptions he is making, then at least everyone will know how others are viewing the future. It is all too common for the planning process to be initiated without first ensuring general agreement as to the framework upon which the plan is to be set.

Much of the planning process is a mechanical exercise done by the accountants, but this is in many ways the least important part. The difficult part is deciding how the company must be directed through the uncertainties of the next few years. This is the responsibility of management, and it is the function for which they are really paid. The successful manager spends most of his time planning, and the rest of it ensuring that other people are putting his plans into action.

The accountant's function in all this is to assist management to see clearly the financial implications of their policies and plans, and to be able to choose the most attractive opportunities from the various alternative courses of action open to them.

The key factor that most boards will consider in planning for the future is the profitability of their company. Profit is a critical factor; no company can survive for long without it. But perhaps profit is more of a means to an end than an end in itself for many modern businesses. The board must still be concerned to ensure that there is sufficient profit to reward shareholders with a dividend, pay employees good wages, and provide funds for capital investment necessary to maintain the company's growth. Profit is an expression of the company's goal. How the profit should be used or distributed is a separate issue that is not within the scope of this book.

When management have produced their forecasts of sales volume, costs and profit, together with capital investment proposals, they must bring them all together in a Master Financial Forecast. This is best done along the lines of funds flow analysis. Where is the company going to generate the funds, and how are these funds to be used? This can be set out in a table similar to the one below:

MASTER FINANCIAL FORECAST, YEAR 1–5

	Year 1	2	3	4	5
Major uses of funds					
Capital investments					
Repayment of loans	—	—	—	—	—
Major sources of funds					
Pre-tax Profit					
Depreciation	—	—	—	—	—
Surplus/Deficit	=	=	=	=	=
Changes in working capital					
Increase/Decrease in stock					
Increase/Decrease in debtors					
Increase/Decrease in cash					
Increase/Decrease in creditors					
Increase/Decrease in taxation					
Increase/Decrease in dividend					
Increase/Decrease in overdraft	—	—	—	—	—
Net change in working capital	=	=	=	=	=
Overall surplus/deficit of funds in year	—	—	—	—	—

A table such as this provides management with the basis for assessing the funds requirements of the company over the next five years if the various forecasts and assumptions used to provide the financial input prove correct. If there is a deficit shown, then management can consider whether or not to raise funds by way of long-term loans or fresh capital issues, or to approach the bank for a short- or medium-term financing agreement.

This table also shows the flexibility of the company in terms of how much of the financial requirements are either found in the area of working capital or could be generated from the changing of the various items there. For example, if there is only a minor deficit in one year, could this be overcome by changing the debtor and stock position rather than borrowing funds? It would also be possible to assess the impact of delaying capital investment programmes by one year on the finance requirements. All these factors, and many more, can be looked at by the management of the company until the final result is agreed and becomes the Five-Year Financial Plan of the company. This is the stated funds flow that management is to achieve over the next five years — a statement of intention, the plan.

Of course, having completed the plan, this does not guarantee that everything will go as predicted. Indeed, the only thing certain is that the plan willl not be met; things will change in a way the company could not predict rendering the plan inoperable. This is the argument that is so often used against formal planning exercises in a company. But it is still beneficial that management have thought about their business in these terms, and have a plan against which to set the changes as they occur. There is a basis for comparison and assessment upon which decisions can be taken which would not be available if planning were ignored. Management is likely to react better to changing circumstances after planning than if none had been done. The financial impact of changes can quickly be fed into the planning table and new decisions and policy made.

The broad long-term planning exercise has been outlined above, but a part of that is the cash budgeting process by which companies can plan for, and monitor, the flow of cash over shorter time periods — normally twelve months.

TABLE 1
SALES AND CASH INFLOW

	December	January	February	March	April
Sales in month	£40,000	60,000	80,000	60,000	40,000

Cash received in month:

	December	January	February	March	April
December	20,000	10,000	10,000		
January		30,000	15,000	15,000	
February			40,000	20,000	20,000
March				30,000	15,000
April					20,000
	£20,000	40,000	65,000	65,000	55,000

(*b*) Other costs and expenses

From the budgets and forecasts the following information was collected as to the various costs and expenses associated with the sales given above:

TABLE 2
COSTS AND EXPENSES

	December	January	February	March	April	4-month total
Materials	£15,000	35,000	30,000	20,000	20,000	(105,000)
Wages	10,000	10,000	20,000	12,000	10,000	(52,000)
Other expenses	10,000	10,000	20,000	10,000	10,000	(50,000)
Capital expenditure			15,000			(15,000)

(i) Materials are paid for in the month following delivery with no discounts allowed.

(ii) Wages are paid one-half in the month incurred and one-half in the following month.

(iii) Other expenses are paid in the month following their being incurred.

(iv) The capital expenditure is for a new machine to be installed and paid for in February.

(*c*) Other information

The company maintains a base stock of raw materials and finished goods of £5,000. This is to be continued into the coming year, and the materials purchases are those necessary to service the sales budget, and maintain the minimum £5,000 stock level.

The company has fixed assets with a written-down value of £100,000 on 31 December. These are depreciated at £30,000 per annum.

The shareholders' interest in the company on 31 December was £97,000. On 31 December the company had a cash balance of £2,000.

From this information it is possible to draft the Balance Sheet as at 31 December, the Cash Budget for the coming four months, and a set of accounts covering this same period.

XYZ LTD BALANCE SHEET, 31 DECEMBER

	£			£
Shareholders' Interest	97,000		Fixed Assests	100,000
Current Liabilities:			Current Assets:	
Creditors:			Stock 5,000	
Materials	15,000		Debtors 20,000	
Wages	5,000		Cash 2,000	27,000
Other	10,000	30,000		
		£127,000		£127,000

XYZ LTD
CASH BUDGET, JANUARY—APRIL

	January	February	March	April	Amount still due
Opening cash balance	2,000	7,000	(3,000)	(4,000)	
Cash from sales	40,000	65,000	65,000	55,000	(35,000)
Total cash available	42,000	72,000	62,000	51,000	
Cash payments:					
Materials	15,000	35,000	30,000	20,000	(20,000)
Wages	10,000	15,000	16,000	11,000	(5,000)
Other	10,000	10,000	20,000	10,000	(10,000)
Capital		15,000			
Total cash out in month	35,000	75,000	66,000	41,000	
Closing cash balance	7,000	(3,000)	(4,000)	10,000	

XYZ LTD
PROFIT AND LOSS ACCOUNT FOR THE FOUR MONTHS
ENDED 30 APRIL

Materials used		105,000	Sales	240,000
Wages		52,000		
Other expenses		50,000		
Depreciation:				
Old plant	10,000			
New plant	1,000	11,000		
Profit		22,000		
		£240,000		£240,000

XYZ L<small>TD</small>
B<small>ALANCE</small> S<small>HEET AS AT</small> 30 A<small>PRIL</small>

Shareholders' Interest:			Fixed Assets:		
December balance	97,000		December balance	100,000	
Profit and Loss	22,000	119,000	February addition	15,000	
Account					
				115,000	
			Depreciation	11,000	104,000

Current Liabilities:			Current Assets:		
Creditors:			Stock	5,000	
Materials (April)	20,000		Debtors (¼ March		
Wages (½ April)	5,000		+ ½ April)	35,000	
Other (April)	10,000	35,000	Cash	10,000	50,000
		£154,000			£154,000

Once the Cash Budget and the pro-forma accounts for the four months have been completed, management can consider their implications. The Profit and Loss Account shows a good profit, and the April Balance Sheet looks healthier than the December one — the working capital situation is much sounder. But the Cash Budget shows that during February and March the company will have to obtain finance of around £4,000 if the budgeted level of activity is to be maintained. This shortage of cash is mainly due to the planned capital investment in the new machine to be made in February. Management can decide whether it is best to obtain an overdraft for the two months from the bank, or to delay the purchase of the machine until April when it will be possible without borrowed money if all goes according to budget.

This much-simplified example highlights the mechanics and the benefits of cash budgeting. If a company can produce a cash budget for the coming twelve months it has available a statement in cash terms of the impact of all its budgeting activity. The planned sales, costs, expenses and capital outlays are all put together to show the cash movement in the company, and to highlight danger points in the year. With this foreknowledge, management can act in plenty of time, either to approach the bank for money, or even raise long-term capital, or to change the pattern and timing of income and expenditure.

In many companies it is not possible to produce a detailed annual cash budget, but it should be possible for every company to draft a shorter period budget, such as three or four months ahead.

Planning the cash movement within a company is a key task, as is deciding how much cash it is advisable to hold. Cash by itself is a wasteful asset. It does not earn any profit — except when placed on deposit, and then it will earn less than if it were employed in the business. How much cash to hold is a difficult theoretical question as well as a practical problem. The use of a cash budget can go a long way to answering it by showing whether the company is maintaining sufficient cash resources throughout the budget, or, if too much cash is expected to be generated, then plans can be made for its profitable investment either in the firm or outside.

One measure than can be used to assess the circulation of cash in the firm is that of cash turnover. This ratio is similar to stock turnover except it is cash that is being dealt with:

$$\text{Cash turnover} = \frac{\text{Sales}}{\text{Opening cash balance}}$$

Different industries will exhibit different cash turnovers and, indeed, firms within the same industry will have different ratios. For example, ICI in 1972 had a cash turnover of 12 whilst Tesco tor 1972 had a turnover of 152. In 1973 the three retailing companies had the following cash turnovers:

	M & S	BHS	Tesco
Cash turnover	29	89	230
Cash as % of current assets (1972 Balance Sheet)	31%	6%	5%
Cash as % of capital employed (1972)	10%	3%	3%

Each company has a different approach to the management of cash and the amount which it is advisable to hold. Tesco is making the best use of cash resources, but in doing so is working to finer financial limits than either of the other two.

As part of the cash budgeting exercise, management will have to consider what is the credit policy to be adopted with customers, and how to monitor the level of debtors. The credit period to be allowed will partly depend on trade custom and partly on the financial state of the company. Once this is decided, it is necessary to ensure that it is followed. One method which is adopted by many firms is to complete each month an age analysis of debtors. This means that each month a statement is prepared showing the age of the debts due to the company.

DEBTOR AGE ANALYSIS REPORT

Total sales debtors at end of month . . . . £

Age of debt	Amount £	% of total
Less than 1 month	. . .	. . .
1 to 2 months	. . .	. . .
2 to 3 months	. . .	. . .
Over 3 months	. . .	. . .
	. . .	100%

With long-term debtors management can be supplied with full information as to why there has been a delay in collecting cash, and what steps are being taken to rectify the situation.

A similar exercise could be conducted in relation to the company's creditors to ensure that correct payment and balances are being maintained.

3.6. Predicting Bankruptcy

The search for the key to unlock the Balance Sheet figures and provide a prediction of impending financial disaster has been for years for accountants as the touchstone was to the alchemists. Somewhere in the Balance Sheet of a company there must be indicators that it is going to go bankrupt next year. It has always been possible to employ funds flow analysis to this end, using historical data and assumptions as to the future to provide some information on this matter. If a company's funds flow has been declining and it is expected to continue to do so, then a simple extrapolation using ordinary Balance Sheet ratios can show when it is likely to become critical, calling for ouside finance or complete reorganisation.

In the late 1960s an American professor, E. I. Altman of New York University, did some research into the question of whether typical Balance Sheet ratios could enable good predictions of bankruptcy to be made. His findings would appear to indicate that there is some basis for a belief that this is possible. Using a computer and a technique known as 'multiple discriminant analysis' — a variation on multiple regression analysis — he produced the following formula, or discriminant function:

$$Z = .012a + .014b + .033c + .006d + .999e$$

where a = working capital/total assets
       b = retained earnings/total assets
       c = earnings before interest and tax/total assets
       d = market value of equity/book value of total debt
       e = sales/total assets.

The first four ratios are all expressed as percentages, and the final one is the asset turnover ratio. In ratio b the retained earnings means the total amount of retained profit appearing in the Balance Sheet, and ratio c measures the pre-tax-and-interest profit for the year as a percentage of total assets. Ratio d measures the 'capitalisation' of the company, that is, the number of shares issued multiplied by their market value divided by the liabilities of the company with the exception of shareholders' interest.

Once the five ratios are calculated and, after being weighted according to the formula, added together, the resulting Z factor can be used as an indicator of the future financial health of the company. If the Z factor is over 3, then the firm is unlikely to go bankrupt in the coming year; if it is under 2, the firm is likely to have severe financial problems in the future.

There does appear to be some basis for taking such prediction methods seriously, and almost certainly within the next few years variations on Altman's formula will be used in credit assessment of companies.

This short section on predicting bankruptcy is intended to show the way in which ratios can be used in conjunction with statistical techniques to provide useful information. As this is an area of research that is certain to continue, it is important that managers know the sort of work that is being done. It has not been possible to do anything like justice to Altman's work here, and for further information reference should be made to the article he wrote in the *Journal of Finance*, vol. XXIII, Sep. 1968, and his book *Corporate Bankruptcy in the United States* (Lexington, 1970).

4 Sources of Business Finance

Every company as it grows will be faced with the problem that it cannot finance its development entirely from its own operations. Its funds requirements will be greater than its funds generation at certain points of time. The question then is how, and where, shall the additional finance be raised?

One experienced financier, when asked about borrowing money, produced the dictum, 'If the money is available, and looks cheap, borrow it even if you don't need it immediately.' Over the last few years, with the experience of inflation, this statement would have stood many companies in good advantage. It is always better to borrow, or arrange to borrow, funds well in advance of their need becoming desperate. A company that only starts looking for finance when it already needs the money is a badly managed company. Chapter 3 outlined the method of longer-range financial planning and the shorter-term cash budgeting which allows management plenty of warning of future funds requirements. This chapter outlines the means by which the financial requirements of companies can be met.

There are two types of finance. There is the short-term requirement for funds, and the need for longer, even permanent, finance. Firstly, there are various sources and types of short-term finance which can be employed by a company having a need for additional finance for a limited period only, and which does not, or cannot, raise long-term finance.

4.1. Short- and Medium-Term Finance
Bank Borrowing
Probably the best known, and most used, source of short-term finance is the bank overdraft. Every company will have

at least one bank account with a U.K. clearing bank, or similar banking institutions which have branches in the High Street.

These banks are in the business of lending money, and in so doing have, over the years, developed a whole range of services which can assist companies of all sizes over their financial problems. In recent years the banks have moved into the medium- to longer-term loan area, and it is now possible to obtain ten-year loans from most of the U.K. banks, but their main emphasis is still on short-term finance.

Theoretically the overdraft is repayable to the bank on demand — this is why it is always shown as a current liability in the Balance Sheet — but in practice this is rarely demanded, or feasible, without winding the company up, although at times during the 'squeeze' in the early 1970s pressure was applied to many firms by their banks to repay or reduce their overdrafts.

The overdraft is the most flexible form of finance there is. With an agreed overdraft limit a company can manage its affairs as it sees fit, and if the whole amount offered is not used, then there is no interest paid on it, and if it is repaid earlier than was expected there is no interest due on the balance that could have been used.

In approaching the bank a company should prepare a detailed cash flow forecast — a cash budget — that will provide the banker with the answer to the main questions he will raise:

How is the money to be used?
How much money is required?
When is the money required?
When will the money be repaid?

This cash budget will be supported by the latest accounts of the company and, from the bank's own records, a history of previous dealings with the bank and details of the individuals concerned in the company.

The banker can then assess the viability of the loan proposal, and offer terms to the company. The bank will first decide how much they feel able to offer, with or without security, and then at what rate of interest. The rate of interest will depend on many factors, but mainly on the degree of risk that the banker associates with the proposal. It will be quoted at a percentage above the ruling bank rate.

The ideal overdraft from the bank's view is what is termed a 'self-liquidating' one, that is, the loan will be repaid out of the continued operations of the business. For example, if the bank allows an overdraft for a few months while a company builds up stocks of finished goods, it will expect to see the overdraft repaid from the proceeds of the sale of these goods at a later date in the year. The overdraft has been self-liquidating.

The overdraft will only be used for short-term situations — though looking at the accounts of many large public companies it is clear that the overdraft forms an almost permanent part of their capital structure.

Given the flexibility of the overdraft facility, to draw and repay at will within an agreed limit, it is probably the easiest and cheapest form of finance open to companies.

Trade Credit

Delaying the payment of creditors is an often used form of short-term finance by individuals as well as companies. A company that decides to adopt this method must always be careful of the long-term consequences. The goodwill of the supplier may be taken to the limit, and produce a reluctance to supply any more materials without immediate payment of all previous bills, and this could be awkward for the company. The reputation for being a bad payer can also be a nuisance to a company, and hamper overall trade relations with suppliers or a local community.

However, there is one factor that companies should always take advantage of, and that is any discounts that are offered. Even a small discount for payment within a few days can be very useful to a company. For example, if a supplier delivers goods valued at £1,000, and offers a discount of 2% if their bill is paid in 30 days, the company should whenever possible take the discount. The reason is that the real rate of discount is much higher than 2%:

$$\frac{£20}{£980} \times \frac{365 \text{ days}}{30 \text{ days}} = 25\% \text{ per annum}$$

Or a simpler method is found by the fact that the annual equivalent of 1% per month is approximately 13% per annum.

The annual rate of interest represents the real advantage the company would be missing if it did not take the available discount. It is also clear from these calculations that companies should be very careful about what discounts they in turn offer customers for prompt payment.

Factoring and Invoice Discounting
The factoring of debtors is the selling of a company's debtors to another firm which maintains the necessary book-keeping records and credit control mechanisms to collect these debts. Invoice discounting is the selling of the company's debtors to release funds tied up in them.

This form of raising short-term finance is just beginning to obtain general acceptance in the U.K. For a long time it was associated with the fact that a company was going bankrupt, or in deep financial crisis, and as a result of this companies were afraid of factoring their debts in case their customers gained the opinion that they were in financial trouble. It is now possible to adopt undisclosed factoring, a method which ensures that the company's customer is unaware that its debt has been sold to another company.

Factoring and invoice discounting release to the company up to 90% of the value of invoices acceptable to the concern being dealt with. This can be a very useful source of immediate funds to a company, though the costs associated with this are 1—3% of sales value, and so much higher than bank overdraft rates.

Bills of Exchange
A bill of exchange is in effect a sort of postdated cheque. It allows a company a certain time to pay the bill together with interest. The company owing the money 'accepts' the bill, by writing 'accepted' on it, and when it comes due for payment (when it matures) the amount plus interest is paid to whoever

holds it. The company who has the right to payment on the bill can sell, or 'negotiate', the bill with a bank or any other person or institution, and in so doing will sell at lower than face value, the bill thus being 'discounted'.

Whilst bills of exchange can only really be used by the larger companies to provide them with a source of funds closely allied in cost to that of bank overdraft facilities, there is no reason why smaller companies dealing with large ones cannot obtain bills of exchange which can then be discounted for cash.

Hire-Purchase

Hire-purchase can be just as attractive to a company as it is to an individual. The total cost of an item need not be paid out all at once, but spread over a longer period of time with weekly or monthly instalments. This spreads the cost of the asset over time, which can be helpful to the company.

Not only is the capital cost of the asset paid, but also an interest charge. The real cost of hire-purchase will vary from firm to firm, but will often be found to be more than double the cost of overdraft facilities. Hire-purchase is therefore quite expensive, but a company using hire-purchase to obtain an asset on its business can, since the 1971 Finance Act, claim tax allowances on it in just the same manner as if the asset were wholly owned.

Leasing

Today almost any plant, machinery, buildings and equipment that a company may need can be leased. This allows companies to consider whether it is better to purchase outright an asset for immediate cash payment or to lease it from a leasing firm. The decision whether to buy or lease assets will depend on the cash flow of the firm, and its other plans. If leased, the asset can be used by the company in just the same manner as if it were purchased, and a regular cash outflow will be experienced as the rental is paid.

Sale and lease-back is a common form of freeing cash from fixed assets into working capital. By this method a company which owns an asset can sell it to an insurance company or finance institution or other concern, and lease it back at an agreed rate. This can free large amounts of cash for the company without in any way altering the use of physical assets.

Merchant Banks and Venture Capital

The merchant banks and other financial institutions are always looking for growing companies which can make profitable use of money to maintain or increase their growth. This is particularly true where the company concerned can use the additional finance to grow to a size that makes an offer of shares to the public possible. This is the provision of venture capital. The firm providing it puts in money to a firm in return for shares or other loan agreements that can be converted in the future into shares with the intention of making a good return once the shares are offered to the public.

This form of finance enables a company to obtain £50,000 to £500,000 on very competitive terms, and at the same time much helpful financial advice from the professionals employed by the lending company. However, a company following this source of funds must expect to release some proportion of its equity in return for the loan, and this can sometimes be unacceptable to the directors.

4.2. Long-Term Finance

Where a company already has a stock exchange quotation it can offer more of its shares to the public to raise further funds to continue the business. There are various methods that can be adopted to do this.

(a) *Public issue.* This method involves the company offering the public its shares, using a prospectus which contains all the information considered necessary by both government legislation and by stock exchange requirements. The shares are offered at a fixed price and the public apply for the number they require.

(b) *Offer for sale.* With a prospectus containing details of the company's history and potential the shares are offered to the public, not by the company, but by one of the financial institutions. The financial institution has purchased all the shares from the company at an agreed price, and then offers them to the public at a higher price. The margin made on the issue replaces the fee which would have been charged for assistance with a public issue. Under this method the company is free from concern in case the issue is not fully taken up by the public.

(*c*) *Placing.* With this method the shares that are to be offered, or the majority of those shares, are sold privately by the financial institutions to its clients. This method is only really suitable for smaller share issues.

(*d*) *Sale by tender.* This is similar to an offer for sale except that there is a minimum price set on the shares, and offers are invited. The person wishing to purchase shares states the price he is willing to pay and the number he requires. The shares are then allocated on the basis of the best bids that will take up all the shares offered.

(*e*) *Rights issue.* With this form of an issue existing shareholders are offered the right to purchase new shares in proportion to their holding of the existing issued shares of the company. The price at which the shares are offered is below the current market price of that class of shares in the company.

Other types of share issue are also met with in studying company financial behaviour, but these are not really concerned with raising funds for operations:

(*f*) *Scrip issue.* Where the company has a high proportion of its shareholders' interest made up of reserves — either retained profit or capital reserves — the dividend that is paid to shareholders can often appear excessive when related to the shares issued rather than their total investment in the company, the shareholders' interest. To change this the company can issue shares to existing shareholders that convert the reserves into shares. This is what is often termed a scrip issue. It is the capitalisation of reserves. It makes no real difference to the shareholders except that they will have more shares, and the company show less reserves.

(*g*) *Share split.* Sometimes a company's shares reach a very high price which makes them difficult to deal in. If a £1 share has a market value of £50, then its marketability can be expected to be limited. Thus, a company may decide to split the £1 share into 50 2p shares. This raises no additional cash for the company, and does not affect the shareholder other than the fact that he now has 50 shares instead of one, and can sell some of his holding more easily than before. It is also possible to reverse this procedure and consolidate a number of small-value shares into one of larger value.

The cost of issuing shares can be quite considerable as there are many points at which professional services must be obtained and paid for. The legal costs must be met, as must the accountant's fees for providing the various special reports necessary, and there is also advertising and printing costs as well as any underwriting commission.

Share issues can be underwritten by an issuing house, that is, a financial institution will guarantee that any shares that are not taken up in the issue will be purchased. For this guarantee they will charge an underwriting commission.

The mechanics of issuing shares are relatively simple. The critical problem is concerned with what sort of shares to issue and, most important, at what price. If the company offers shares at too low a price, then it will have lost an opportunity to raise funds, and if the price is too high it may not raise as much as was expected. If a company and its advisers have got the issue price correct, it can be expected that the dealings in the shares on the stock exchange immediately after the issue will be at 5—10% above the issue price.

4.3 Types of Capital

Having discussed the various means by which shares can be issued to increase the funds available in the company, it is necessary to discover what sort of shares and debentures can be so issued.

Equity Capital

The equity capital of a company is made up of its ordinary shares. These are the shares that have a right to participate in the profits of the company by way of dividends that are

decided by the company's directors. They have no rights to a
fixed return, and the dividend will depend on the profits
available for distribution after the directors have made all
appropriations they see fit.

The ordinary shareholders will only receive payment of a
dividend after all other shareholders have been satisfied by
payment of their due dividend. There may be several classes
of ordinary shares:

- Preferred Ordinary
- Deferred Ordinary
- Founders' shares
- A Ordinary
- B Ordinary

These types of shares may have different voting rights.

When funds are raised by issue of ordinary shares the only
costs will be those of the actual issue. There is no
requirement to continue a fixed rate of dividend as there is
with other forms of capital. If a company does not pay a
dividend, then it will retain the profit for further growth, and
the market value of the ordinary shares can be expected to
rise to compensate for the lack of dividend.

The Balance Sheet of the company will show what is the
authorised number and nominal value of ordinary shares that
may be issued as well as the actual issued shares on that date.
This value for the ordinary shares is the 'par value'. Thus, a
company that has ordinary shares with a nominal value of £1
each has ordinary shares of £1 par value.

Fixed Capital

Preference shares have declined in attractiveness over the last
ten years. The reason for this decline in popularity is quite
simple. The owner of preference shares will receive a fixed
rate of dividend on his investment, and under conditions of
inflation this is not an attractive proposition. The preference
shareholders will be paid their dividend before the ordinary
shareholder, and in the case of a liquidation they have prior
claim to repayment before all other shareholders. There are
various forms of preference share:

(a) *Cumulative Preference*. These shares have the right to have any dividend not paid in one year carried over and added to the dividend due in the following year.

(b) *Participating Preference*. These have the right to share in profits not only with their own fixed dividend, but also after the ordinary shareholders have had a certain level of dividend.

(c) *Redeemable Preference*. These are shares that can be re-purchased by the company. Certain funds alone can be used for this purpose — profits otherwise available for dividend funds from a new issue of shares specifically for this purpose. When redemption is made out of profits, an amount equal to the nominal value of the shares must be placed in a Capital Redemption Reserve Fund, and this fund can be used to make a scrip issue (Section 58, 1948 Companies Act).

(d) *Convertible Preference*. These shares can be converted into ordinary shares at some future date, and at an agreed price.

As preference shares have declined in use, debentures have increased. These are more flexible than preference shares, and also cheaper:

(a) *Floating Debenture*. This is a loan which is secured by a floating charge on all the company's assets.

(b) *Fixed Debenture*. This is a loan which is secured on some particular asset, or assets, of the company — usually land and buildings. This means that the company cannot dispose of that asset at will; it must either pay off the debenture or obtain permission from the debenture holder.

(c) *Convertible Debenture*. This is a debenture which has the right to be converted into ordinary shares at some future date and at an agreed price. This is a very popular method of providing venture capital to smaller firms. The institution providing the finance can obtain a reasonable rate of interest on the loan, and also participate in the equity of the company when it reaches an acceptable size.

The main reason for more debentures being issued currently rather than preference shares is that the interest on a debenture is allowable against tax whereas preference dividends are not.

4.4. Capital Gearing

The term 'capital gearing', or 'leverage', is used to describe the relationship between the fixed-interest capital and the equity capital of a company. A company can be described as being 'highly geared' or 'low geared'. A highly geared company is one which has a high proportion of fixed-interest capital compared with equity capital, and a low-geared company has the reverse situation, that is, little fixed capital compared with ordinary shares, and reserves that form the shareholders' interest.

As with most of the other terms so far discussed in this book, there are many alternative definitions. Capital gearing can also mean:

$$\text{Gearing} = \frac{\text{Ordinary share capital}}{\text{Preference share capital}}$$

$$\text{or} \quad = \frac{\text{Long-term finance and loans}}{\text{Total capital employed}}$$

$$\text{or} \quad = \frac{\text{Long-term debt}}{\text{Equity capital} + \text{long-term debt}}$$

To illustrate the concept, and the importance, of capital gearing, consider the three firms below:

	A	B	C
Ordinary share capital	3	2	0.5
Reserves	1	1	0.5
Fixed-interest capital	1	2	4.0
	£5	£5	£5

Using the most common measure of gearing — comparing the shareholders' interest (not just the ordinary share capital) with fixed-interest capital — the figures for these three firms are:

	A	B	C
Gearing ratio	0.25	0.67	4.0
Gearing	Low	Medium	High

The rationale for gearing in financing a company is that if fixed-interest capital is raised, and can be used to earn a return in excess of the interest charge, then this goes to the ordinary shareholders of the company.

Thus, if companies A, B and C earn profits of £1 in the year, and the fixed-interest capital is at 10%, then:

	A	B	C
Profit	1.0	1.0	1.0
Interest at 10%	0.1	0.2	0.4
Available for ordinary shares	£0.9	£0.8	£0.6

Thus, with the same profit, but different gearing, these firms produce varying profits for the ordinary shareholders of the company. This can be expressed as earning per share:

	A	B	C
Number of ordinary shares	3	2	0.5
Profit	£0.9	£0.8	£0.6
Earnings per share	£0.3	£0.4	£1.2

It is clear that the higher the gearing, the better the earnings per share for the ordinary shareholders. But with high gearing there is the risk of one year of low profits making it impossible to pay out all the required interest, and so management must strike an acceptable balance. If in the case of companies A, B and C profit in the year were to drop to £0.3, the earnings per share would become £0.07, £0.05 and —£0.2 respectively. With the high gearing in company C there would be a negative return to the ordinary shareholders because the profit would not cover the interest requirements of the year.

One way of expressing this is to compare the fixed-interest charge with the total profit earned before deducting that interest charge. For the three companies this is:

		A	B	C
Profit before interest	=	£1.0	£1.0	£1.0
Fixed-interest charge		£0.1	£0.2	£0.4
Times interest is covered =		10	5	2.5

A company which is making use of gearing must leave itself scope for the fluctuations in profit, and thus an interest cover of at least three or four times should be allowed, otherwise the company is likely to be too highly geared for safety. If a company decides that a cover of five times is best for its needs, then this figure can be used to discover what is the maximum level of fixed interest the company can pay, and thereby the maximum amount of fixed-interest capital that the company should raise.

Another aspect of gearing is the amount of the company's finance that is being raised from current liabilities. This can be measured by the ratio:

$$\frac{\text{Current liabilities}}{\text{Shareholders' interest}} \quad \text{or} \quad \frac{\text{Current liabilities}}{\text{Net worth} + \text{Long-term finance}}$$

A company that has a high ratio here can be assumed to have very little cushion against short-term fluctuations to fall back upon. If the maximum amount of credit is already being taken, and creditors stretched to the limit, then no more funds can be obtained from current liabilities if the need for short-term finance should arise.

5 The Stock Exchange

In Chapter 4 the various methods of raising finance were considered, together with the alternative forms of short-, medium- and long-term capital open to a company. In this chapter an outline is provided of the way in which institutions and individuals who influence or constitute the financial markets assess a company's performance. Accordingly, the more commonly used ratios are discussed in relation to the nature of the share market.

5.1. Financial Information Required

In assessing the current state of a company's financial health, and its historic performance record, the ratios discussed in Chapter 2 are of obvious importance, for they provide an indication of past success, and some early warning of future problems. But there are in addition a number of key ratios used by analysts, both amateur and professional, of company stocks. These are the ratios which appear, for instance, in the share information tables of the *Financial Times*, and other national newspapers and journals.

These ratios are made up of three pieces of information which are available from a company's Annual Report, and one external piece of information. The Balance Sheet provides:

— the number of shares outstanding
— the net income for the year
— the dividend declared by the directors

As well as these facts, the market price of the stock is needed. This is the price at which the shares of the company are changing hands on the stock market.

These basic building blocks in financial ratio analysis require some further comment, for all can be defined in

103

different ways, and it is easy to be misled if the information is taken at face value and applied as a performance yardstick without checking its basis.

First, the number of shares outstanding is the number of shares actually issued by the company, which is not necessarily the same as the number of shares the company is authorised to issue. In the company's Balance Sheet this will be made clear under the section dealing with the net worth of the company. But the number of shares issued may be increased or decreased in the period following the publication of the Annual Report. A company may retire some of its own stock, for whatever reason, or there may be a stock split or scrip issue, or stock options or conversions may be exercised.

Under a stock option scheme, the employees of a company may be given the option in the future to purchase shares at a predetermined price, the intention being that if the company is successful through the work of its employees, the share price will rise allowing a net capital gain to be made when the options are exercised. The number of shares issued under any such scheme is normally small in relation to the total stock issued.

A similar scheme may involve 'convertible paper' such as preference shares or debentures. In such cases the system is rather similar to the stock option, in that it allows for the purchase into common stock (ordinary shares) at a future date, but these issues may be made to the public as well as those institutions mentioned in the previous chapter. In return for putting up capital, the investor receives a debenture (which contains an obligation on behalf of the company to pay a fixed rate of interest) or preferred shares, which also contain the requirement for a fixed rate of interest before, or in preference to, the common stockholders. It is changes in the balance between various forms of finance due to the exercising of convertible rights that the investment analyst must check in calculating the number of shares issued by the company at any given time.

The second piece of information from the Annual Report is the net income or profit for the year. This was defined in some detail in Chapters 1 and 2. The 'net income' should be taken as net not only of debenture interest, which will have been deducted before corporation tax, but also of preferred stock dividends, which are payable after deduction of tax (see also Appendix 2, pp. 198—200 below). For in analysing common stock prices, one is concerned only with the income attributable to, or earned by, that common stock.

Likewise, if comparisons are made between several years, or between companies, care must be exercised to ensure that such comparison uses common factors; like must be compared with like. The net income for a period may be affected by unusual or non-recurring items. Such items may result from an unusually large bad debt as a major customer is liquidated, or a capital gain on the sale of an asset.

The third piece of information is the dividend that the directors have declared for the year. Most large companies nowadays declare interim dividends, sometimes quarterly, sometimes half-yearly. These are aggregated to provide the total annual dividend.

Finally, there is the market price — the price at which shares are traded on the stock exchange. Most share prices, for reasons discussed later, undergo considerable fluctuations during any year. It is these fluctuations that make it necessary to publish share prices daily for the general public, and to monitor them continually on the stock exchange. To assist appreciation of share price movements, most share tables provide details of the current year's lowest and highest price for any particular share.

5.2. Basic Stock Exchange Ratios
To allow illustration of the various stock exchange ratios used to assess company performance, the company Hedgebet Ltd is used as an example. Hedgebet has 50,000 shares authorised, and has issued 40,000. The net of tax income for the current year is £80,000, and a dividend of £1 has been declared on the 40,000 ordinary shares issued. Thus, £40,000 of the net of tax income is paid to the shareholders, and £40,000 retained in the company. The current market price of the shares is £16 each.

The first ratio to be considered is that of earnings per share. This ratio shows what income was available for the payment of the ordinary share dividend, and is found by dividing the net income by the total number of shares issued. For Hedgebet Ltd, this is:

$$\frac{\text{Net income}}{\text{Number of shares issued}} = \frac{£80,000}{40,000} = £2 \text{ per share}$$

This figure of earnings per share (EPS) is used in the calculation of a further ratio, that of the price-earnings ratio. This ratio has been used for many years in America, and over the last ten years has become widely used in the U.K. as a key financial ratio both for company assessment and financial planning. It is calculated by taking the market price of the share, and dividing this by the earnings per share. For Hedgebet Ltd, this is:

$$\frac{\text{Market price of share}}{\text{Earnings per share}} = \frac{£16}{£2} = 8$$

The price — earnings ratio (P/E) is a very important one. It enables comparison to be made between all companies, between companies within an industry group, and between industries. In simple terms, the lower the P/E the lower the market's valuation of the share's future performance.

It is useful to know the number of times that the dividend is covered by the net income. This is referred to as the 'times covered' or 'earnings cover' ratio. The ratio is calculated by dividing the available net income by the amount of the dividend distribution. For Hedgebet Ltd, this is:

$$\frac{\text{Available income}}{\text{Dividend}} = \frac{£80,000}{£40,000} = 2 \text{ times covered}$$

If a company were to distribute all the available income to shareholders as dividend, this might look attractive for investment purposes in the immediate period, but it would not be a sound strategy to adopt. If profitability were to suffer, the company would find it difficult to maintain operations or pay dividends. It is expected that companies will retain at least some of their income in reserves.

It is important to assess the annual income accruing from an investment, and for this the yield is calculated. This can be done by taking the inverse of the P/E ratio which gives the 'capitalisation rate' or 'earnings yield'. This is the rate at which the market is capitalising the value of current earnings. In the example of the Hedgebet company:

$$\frac{\text{Earnings per share}}{\text{Market price of share}} = \frac{1}{\text{P/E ratio}} = \frac{1}{8} = 12.5\%$$

This ratio enables a comparison to be made between shares and other interest-bearing investments. For the 12.5% can be regarded as a form of interest earned by the stock. Note that it is not necessarily the historic interest rate (which would be the return based on the price at which an individual had purchased the stock), and also that it differs from interest-bearing investments in that with common stock all income is not usually distributed in dividends by the company.

The price—earnings ratio and the capitalisation rate, being ratios, are relative measures. If Hedgebet's earnings increase in the following year and the market price of the shares increases commensurately to take account of this, the P/E ratio and the capitalisation rate can remain the same, even though shareholders who have retained their shares since the previous year will have benefited from the increase in share price (in that the value of their holding will have increased) and from dividends (assuming that the company maintains its dividend policy).

For instance, if net income rises to £120,000, with the same number of shares outstanding, the earnings per share will be £3. If the market price rises proportionately the price will become £24, but the price-earnings ratio will remain the same as in the previous year, at 8 (£24/£3). The capitalisation rate will also remain constant at 12.5%.

This underlines a key point about share information tables. They are always expressed in terms of current prices, for current buyers and sellers. With the Hedgebet company one will have to invest £24 to earn (assuming that earnings are the same next year) £3. In the previous year an investment of £16 provided income of £2. But in effect the investor buying a share at £16 last year has earned £1.50 dividend on the investment, and seen its value increase on the stock market by £8. The point that should be noted in this is that the return on investment in shares consists of two components, the increase (or decrease) in the share's price, and the dividend payout. In the case of Hedgebet it could be said that the market was possibly undervaluing the share price or putting a high-risk valuation on its earnings.

If the share price is multiplied by the number of shares in issue, the 'capitalisation' of the company is produced — the total value of the issued shares as valued by the market. For Hedgebet this would be:

Issued shares x Market price = 40,000 x £16 = £640,000

The market capitalisation of quoted companies appears in the Monday morning national newspapers (as there has been no dealing in shares since Friday and so space is available in the share information tables). However, it should be remembered that the market in shares is the point at which willing buyers meet willing sellers. Were all the shareholders in a company to try to sell their shares in a company at the same time, the price would be likely to plummet, considerably reducing the market capitalisation of that company.

One final measure relating to dividend payments is the 'dividend yield'. This is found by dividing the dividend per share by the market price of the share. For Hedgebet, this is:

$$\frac{\text{Dividend per share}}{\text{Market price of share}} = \frac{£1}{£16} = 6.25\%$$

It can be seen that this is exactly one-half of the earnings yield (12.5%), which is to be expected as the dividend payout is one-half of the net income. The dividend yield enables companies to be compared in terms of their payout policy. This can be important, as some companies adopt a policy of regular and constant dividend payouts.

The reader should now be able to understand the various columns appearing in a typical share information table. These tables which appear in the national press have the following format:

£	£		Closing		Dividend	Times	Gross	P/E
High	*Low*	*Stock*	*£ price*	*+/–*	*%*	*covered*	*yield %*	*ratio*
20	12	Hedgebet	16	–	100	2	12.5	8

5.3. Other Information Needs

A potential investor in a share requires not only the information set out in the stock exchange ratios in the previous section, but also other more general information, before deciding upon investment. The historical performance of the company and the dividend policy being adopted will be studied, as will the Chairman's Statement in the latest available Annual Report which should give some indication as to the future prospects of the company — though it is not realistic to expect any chairman to forecast bankruptcy in the coming year, even though there may well be a high probability of this event for his company.

The industry in which the company operates must also be considered. If this industry is likely to suffer in the future, then this can make shares in companies operating in the industry less attractive. Share prices can also be expected to move in respect of industrial unrest, imports, government legislation and the general state of the economy. Very few shares have escaped the gloom of December 1973. All these factors must be considered by the investor before taking his decision.

The requirements of the individual investor will also be important in the decisions taken. A simple grid can show this:

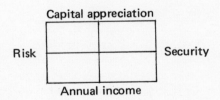

The attitudes and requirements of the investor will be reflected in the investment decisions taken. A person requiring a steady, secure annual income is unlikely to choose the same investment opportunities as a person willing to take risks in order to make large capital gains.

5.4. Stock Exchange Terminology

Finally, a short explanation of stock exchange terminology is provided. The stock exchange is the market where stocks and shares are bought and sold, and where, as a result, the prices of stocks and shares are decided. The stockbrokers deal in stocks and shares for their clients, and make a living by taking a commission on each transaction they undertake. The stockbroker deals with the public on the one hand and with the stockjobbers on the other. The stockjobbers tend to specialise in one particular section of the market, buying and selling shares on their own behalf and then setting the prices at which they are willing to sell to other jobbers and stockbrokers. The jobber makes his profit on the difference between the purchase and selling price of the stocks and shares he deals in. This is known as the 'jobber's turn'.

Other common terminology of the stock market is:

Bulls — who buy stocks and shares hoping they will rise in price and be sold at a profit.

Stags — apply for shares which are new to the market hoping to be able to sell them immediately after they receive their allotment and make a profit (because once the shares are available they are popular enough to be sold at a higher level than their original issue price).

Bears — are the opposite of bulls. They sell stocks and shares they do not own hoping that their prices will fall by the time they have to be delivered to the purchaser.

6 Capital Investment Appraisal

When a company decides to invest some its available funds in a new machine or building, or to develop and launch a new product, the results of this decision will be with the company for a long time into the future. The company will have to live with the results of its investment decisions and, if the decision has proved bad, then this can be a painful process. Most companies will have only limited funds available for such capital investment opportunities, and must make the best use they can of these funds by allocating them wisely. It is these two factors that make the investment decision such an important one in any firm. There are limited resources available and the results of their investment will have a long-term impact on the firm's success.

This chapter deals with the basic techniques of investment appraisal and their application in typical investment situations, and with the problems of risk and uncertainty associated with such decisions.

6.1. The Investment Decision

Before looking at the mechanics of the investment decision, it is important to establish that the calculation of the anticipated profitability of an investment is only one part of the decision process. The final profit calculation is founded on the various estimates, forecasts and guesses that have gone to provide the cash flow figures. These are the income and expenditure data for the project which will be used to assess its profitability, and to compare it against other investment opportunities open to the firm.

If a company were considering launching a new product, it would have to consider very carefully several factors before

111

reaching the stage of assessing its profitability:

(*a*) *The Market*
   What is the size of the market?
   How stable a market is it?
   How difficult is it for competition to enter the market?
   Who are the customers?
   What are the customers' needs?

(*b*) *The Market Growth Potential*
   What growth pattern is expected in the market?
   What share of the market will the firm attain?
   What are the export possibilities?
   How long to establish customer acceptance of the
      product?
   What impact will the new product have on existing ones?

(*c*) *Product Marketing Potential*
   What will customers require of the new product?
   How will the new product be promoted?
   Will the new product fit into the firm's market image?
   What impact will the product have on existing markets?

(*d*) *Internal Factors*
   Has the company the necessary competence in this field?
   Are raw materials readily available?
   What plant facilities will be required for production?
   Can existing distribution channels be used?

(*e*) *Financial Factors*
   What capital will be required for fixed assets?
   What capital will be required for working capital?
   What will be the investment life?
   What will be the revenue and costs of the new product?
   What will be the cost of raising the capital?

Having considered these factors and obtained answers to
the questions raised, the company is in a position to start
assessing the financial viability of the new venture. The
financial calculations depend on the groundwork done by the

sales department in forecasting volume, and the manufacturing department in forecasting costs and expenses necessary to achieve the physical sales objectives. If, as is quite common, these estimates and forecasts are only considered to have an accuracy of ±10% or more, there is little point in doing financial calculations to four decimal places. The company will want an assessment on the return the investment will provide, but anyone providing an answer that 'The rate of return on this project will be 18.4725%' is being unrealistically accurate. The mathematical calculations may be correct to four decimal places, but the input data will have such varying degrees of uncertainty that a simple answer such as 18.4725% is impossibly precise.

The aim of investment appraisal is to provide management with the basis upon which to take important and far-reaching decisions about where to allocate their limited resources, and still ensure the continued profitability of the company.

Some of the more common methods of assessing capital investment opportunities are discussed below, but it must be remembered that it is more often than not the input data that are critical to the calculations, not the particular technique adopted for final appraisal.

6.2. Methods of Appraisal

Payback

The quickest method of assessing a capital investment proposal is to see how long it will take for the project to repay the necessary investment to commence it. This is the payback method, measuring the time from initial investment to recovery of that amount from the project.

Payback is widely used by companies as a back-up to other appraisal techniques. The reason for this is simple. If a company has limited financial resources available, it will be most interested in those projects that give the quickest turnround of its funds. Indeed, at times in the larger companies payback is the critical factor in allocating funds to competing projects. If a company knows it is going to require a large amount of cash in the near future — having done a detailed cash budget as outlined in Chapter 3 — then only projects that can return their capital before this time may be considered. This may occur even though more profitable, but longer-term, investment may thereby be rejected.

In the example below there is information on three projects together with their payback periods:

	A	B	C
Capital outlay	£1,000	1,000	4,000
Profit before depreciation:			
Year 1	200	800	1,500
2	400	600	1,500
3	600	400	1,500
4	800	200	1,500
5	–	–	1,500
	£2,000	2,000	7,500
Payback period	2⅔ years	2¼ years	2⅔ years

On the basis of payback, project B is the best with 2¼ years. But if only projects A and C were available, then it would have been impossible to distinguish between them on the basis of payback. They both provide a 2⅔-year payback period.

The payback can be used as a coarse sieve to bring up only those proposals that are worthy of further consideration where cash is a limiting factor not only today but also in the future. However, the payback period does not give any weight to what happens after the payback period. For example, if project A in the fifth year were to provide a pre-depreciation profit of £1,000, this would not alter its assessment under the payback method.

Average Rate of Return
It is possible to calculate the average rate of return of each of the three projects A, B and C. If depreciation is assumed to be on the straight-line method, then for projects A and B depreciation would be £250 each year, and for C £800 per year. The average rate of return for each project is:

	A	B	C
Total net profit	£1,000	1,000	3,500
Life of project in years	4	4	5
Average annual profit	£250	250	700
Average rate of return	25%	25%	20%

In this case it would be impossible to choose between projects A and B as both have a 25% return on capital invested. The reason why the rate of return method is incapable of distinguishing between A and B is because it assumes there is a uniform profit over the life of the project, and yet this is clearly not the case. Project A has the reverse profit flow of project B.

The rate of return method is unacceptable as an investment appraisal technique as it ignores the timing of the cash flow, and also uses the accounting definition of profit as its basis — that is, after charging the depreciation of the investment.

The Time Value of Money: Discounting

The main criticism of the two methods of investment appraisal so far illustrated is that they ignore the timing of the cash flows resulting from the investment decision. The average rate of return of projects A and B is 25%. But which one is most acceptable to the company — or to any individual? Surely it would be B because the timing of the income is so much better. The greatest income is in the first year in project B, whilst in project A it is in the last year. It is always better to get the cash in quickly. Whilst this is what the payback method measures, it is also important to assess the cash flow timing after the payback period for a full appreciation of the investment opportunity.

To bring into the assessment of capital investment proposals the time value of money, all that is required is an understanding of compound interest. Assume that a sum is invested at a fixed rate of interest for a fixed period. The annual interest is added to the initial sum in the first year; in the second year, interest is paid on the initial sum and on the first year's interest, and so on. Interest is paid on interest — it is compounded.

The concept of compound interest has been known for a long time — certainly in Babylon almost four thousand years ago — and it was used for loan interest calculations in the fifteenth and sixteenth centuries in Europe. Conceptual complexities have never prevented people from making money.

An example of the sort of arithmetic that most of today's

managers did at their school desks many years ago is:

What would £1,000 invested at 10% compound interest be worth at the end of five years?

There are two ways of working this problem out. The first is to tackle it the long way round:

Year   1 = £1,000 + £100 = £1,100
        2 = £1,100 + £110 = £1,210
        3 = £1,210 + £121 = £1,331
        4 = £1,331 + £133 = £1,464
        5 = £1,464 + £146 = £1,610

This shows that at the end of five years the £1,000 has become £1,610. There is also a shorter way using the formula:

$$\text{Final value} = \text{Amount invested}$$
$$(1 + \text{Rate of interest})^{\text{number of years}}$$
$$= £1,000 (1 + 0.1)^5$$
$$= £1,610$$

Using the data in another way, one can say that if the prevailing rate of interest is 10% per annum, then £1,610 in five years' time is worth only £1,000 today. The formula of compound interest can be used to solve questions such as:

What is the present value of £2,000 to be received at the end of two years with a 10% per annum interest rate?

$$\text{Present value} = \frac{\text{Final value}}{(1 + \text{Rate of interest})^{\text{number of years}}}$$

$$= \frac{£2,000}{(1 + 0.1)^2}$$

$$= £1,653$$

This shows that if £1,653 is invested (the present value) at 10% compound interest, it will reach the value of £2,000 at the end of two years. Thus, if a company were offered the chance of receiving £2,000 in two years' time, and 10% is the ruling rate of interest, it would not be willing to pay more than £1,653 today for the opportunity.

This is discounting — compound interest in reverse — and there are sets of tables which provide the necessary discount factors to facilitate calculations. To illustrate their application, if a company wishes to provide £1,000 per year for the next five years, to be paid at the end of the year to their best apprentice, how much must they invest today to ensure its availability each year? If the interest rate is 10%, then using the 10% columns in the tables at the end of the book the following discount factors can be obtained:

	10%	Present value
Year 1	0.9091 x £1,000 =	£909.1
2	0.8264 x £1,000 =	£826.4
3	0.7513 x £1,000 =	£751.3
4	0.6830 x £1,000 =	£683.0
5	0.6209 x £1,000 =	£620.9
		£3,790.7

When the discount factors are multiplied by the sum involved (£1,000), this provides the present values which, when totalled, show that £3,790.7 must be invested at 10% interest to provide £1,000 per annum prize. This can be shown:

	Year 1	2	3	4	5	Total
Amount invested/ balance	£3,790.7	3,169.8	2,486.8	1,735.5	909.0	
Interest at 10%	£379.1	317.0	248.7	173.5	91.0	1,209.3
	£4,169.8	3,486.8	2,735.5	1,909.0	1,000.0	
Apprentice prize paid	£1,000.0	1,000.0	1,000.0	1,000.0	1,000.0	1,000.0
Balance carried forward	£3,169.8	2,486.8	1,735.5	909.0	—	5,000.0

If this example is changed into a decision to purchase a new machine which will cost £3,790 to install and will provide £1,000 per year labour and material savings for the company, then it can be seen that this investment will return

10% to the company over the five-year life of the machine, and will recover the capital cost of £3,790. The £1,000 per year savings can be split into the straight-line depreciation change of £758, and 'profit' of £242. The £242 for the five-year life of the machine provides £1,210 which is the same as the interest total £1,209.3 in the original example.

If the savings or profit from the introduction of the new machine had been £1,200 per year, the present value of the five years' cash flows would have been:

Year 1	£1,200 x 0.9091 =	£1,091
2	£1,200 x 0.8264 =	£992
3	£1,200 x 0.7513 =	£902
4	£1,200 x 0.6830 =	£820
5	£1,200 x 0.6209 =	£745
Present value		£4,550

When this £4,550 is compared with the cost of £3,790, it can be seen to be greater by £760. It has a positive net present value when discounted at 10%. This shows that the investment is returning a rate of interest or profit greater than 10%.

To discover the actual rate of return it is necessary to choose various discount rates until by trial and error the correct rate is found to bring the present value to equal the cost of £3,790.

Discounting the £1,200 at 15% gives a present value of £4,020 which shows the rate is higher still. Discounting at 20% provides a value of £3,590 which shows the rate is too high. Using 17% gives £3,840 and 18% £3,750. Thus, the rate of return of the project is just under 18%.

Where a company has the opportunity for several capital investment projects, but limited funds, it is necessary to rank the choices in order of 'best' return of investment. If the cost of capital to the firm is known, then this may be used as the discount rate, and any projects that have a negative net present value at this rate can be rejected — they are returning less than the cost of capital and so are not profitable.

Where the capital involved in the projects is different, then it is necessary to take these differences into account in the choice. One way of doing this is to use a ratio which relates size of return to the amount of investment:

$$\text{Acceptability index} = \frac{\text{Present value of cash flow}}{\text{Capital outlay}}$$

This ratio will highlight the difference, for instance, between a project which costs £2,000 and has a present value of £3,000, and a project which costs £20,000 and has a present value of £21,000. The ratios are 1.5 and 1.05 respectively.

6.3. Practical Applications
Having covered briefly the concept of discounting, it is now possible to consider what information is necessary in practice for its application, and what benefits discounted cash flow (DCF) analysis can provide.

The input to the calculations is the cash inflow and outflow associated with the capital investment opportunity. It is really the matching of cash out against cash in over the life of the investment and relating this cash flow back to the initial capital outlay. As has already been shown, depreciation is ignored in discounting. The return from a project is calculated before any depreciation charges are deducted, and if in the accounting process depreciation has been charged, it must be added back to provide the cash inflow of the project.

The cash flow that is discounted in a project evaluation is made up as follows:

	£
Income or savings in the year	
less Cost and expenses paid in year	
Taxation paid in year	
Cash flow for year	£

Taxation is a most important factor in investment appraisal and must be deducted in the year in which it is paid, not the year in which it is incurred. This will incorporate all taxation allowances on the capital equipment involved, as this is a tax saving which increases the actual cash inflow of the project.

Where a project requires not only capital investment but also the provision of working capital to enable operations to begin and continue, then this must be included in the cost of the project.

To illustrate the application of discounted cash flow techniques to investment appraisal, a simple example is provided:

A company has estimated demand for an item and now faces the decision of whether it is better to install one large machine which will meet requirements for the next ten years, but run under capacity for a few years, or to buy a small machine which will cover requirements for five years and then add another small machine which with the original will satisfy the remaining five years' demand.

The large machine costs £79,000 and has annual operating costs of £2,000. The small machines cost £50,000 and have operating costs of £1,000 per year. All the machines have estimated lives of ten years.

Which is the better alternative for the company?

The first step in this situation is to set out the costs associated with each alternative:

		2 small machines	*1 large machine*
Capital outlay		£50,000	£79,000
Year	1	1,000	2,000
	2	1,000	2,000
	3	1,000	2,000
	4	1,000	2,000
	5	1,000	2,000
	6	52,000	2,000
	7	2,000	2,000
	8	2,000	2,000
	9	2,000	2,000
	10	2,000	2,000
		£115,000	£99,000

If only the aggregate cash outflow were considered, it would be best if the company purchased one large machine immediately. However, the timing of the cash outflows must be considered. If it is assumed that the company has a cost of capital of 10%, then the present values of the two cash flows are:

	2 small machines	1 large machine
Capital outlay	£50,000	£ 79,000
10 years' outgoings discounted at 10%	£36,100	12,300
	£86,100	£91,300

When the present values of the costs are compared, it can be seen that the purchase of two small machines provides the lower sum. As it is cost that is being considered, and not profit, then it is best to minimise the present value and install two small machines. This would also have the added attraction — which cannot be quantified here — of allowing more flexibility to management. They may find that their estimates of demand are inaccurate and that there is no need for a second machine or that they wish to install the second machine earlier. If, for example, the second machine were added in the fourth year, then the present value of the alternative would be £90,200, which is almost the same as the cost of installing the larger machine. With this knowledge management can assess the situation. As long as the second machine is not to be purchased before year 5, it is best to go for the two small machines. But, as in most investment decisions, attention is focused not on the calculations of discounting but on the input data to those calculations. How certain is management that the estimates are accurate? Some of the methods for improving decision-making under conditions of uncertainty are discussed later in this chapter.

Where a project has a constant stream of income or costs it is possible to use a short-cut method for calculating the present value of this. In the case of the large machine there is a constant £2,000 per year cost for the ten years' life of the machine. This has a present value of:

Year	1	£2,000 x 0.909 =	£1,818
	2	£2,000 x 0.826 =	1,652
	3	£2,000 x 0.751 =	1,502
	4	£2,000 x 0.683 =	1,366
	5	£2,000 x 0.621 =	1,242
	6	£2,000 x 0.564 =	1,128
	7	£2,000 x 0.513 =	1,026
	8	£2,000 x 0.467 =	934
	9	£2,000 x 0.424 =	848
	10	£2,000 x 0.386 =	772
		6.144	£12,288

The £12,288 present value is of a constant annual payment of £2,000. If the discount factors are added they total 6.144, and if £2,000 is multiplied by this it provides £12,288. There are special tables which provide these factors in the case of constant cash flows. They save the tedium of doing the individual calculations, but where these are not at hand it is always simpler to add the discount factors for the relevant number of years and do a single multiplication to obtain the present value. (A sample of annuity tables is given in Appendix 4.)

The Cost of Capital
In the above example it was assumed that the company had a cost of capital of 10%. That is, the cost of raising the necessary finance for the project was 10%; that is the interest that would have to be paid to the bank to borrow the money. Where a project is to generate income it is essential that it be able to return at least the cost of capital to the company; otherwise it will be losing money.

Investment proposals can be discounted at the cost of capital rate to see if they have a positive net present value. If so, this indicates that they make a greater return than the cost of providing the necessary finance. This will provide a quick coarse sieve, in that projects which cannot produce a positive net present value when discounted at the cost of capital rate need not be considered further. The cost of capital represents the minimum level of return acceptable on investments by a company.

With any company it is not sufficient to say that the cost of capital for discounting purposes is the rate paid to the bank for borrowing, or that if there is cash in the bank the cost of capital is zero. Companies obtain their funds from a whole series of sources as was shown in Chapter 3, and these all have different costs.

The company will have share capital and reserves — the shareholders' interest, upon which dividends will be paid. There will be loan capital upon which interest must be paid, and other short-term liabilities which have a cost to the company. One method of arriving at the cost of capital to a company is to take the weighted average cost. This involves taking each source of funds and allocating an interest cost to it, and then weighting this cost in proportion to the amount each source makes of the whole.

Another method is to calculate the rate of return that the company is making currently and use this as the minimum acceptance rate for future projects.

There are many theoretical problems in defining a satisfactory cost of capital, and these can be found in any of the numerous books concentrating on capital budgeting and investment appraisal. The intention in this chapter is merely to make the manager aware that he must have some indication of the cost of capital in his firm if full benefit is to be obtained from the use of discounted cash flow analysis.

6.5. Risk and Uncertainty in the Investment Decision

All investment decisions made by companies are concerned with the future. Capital is invested in a project now for future returns, so there is always a degree of uncertainty associated with the cash flows upon which the decisions are based. Except in very unusual circumstances, it is impossible to be certain what the situation will be five years after an investment decision is made. If the input data to the investment decision are poor, then the chances of making the correct decision are greatly reduced.

There is no way of ensuring good investment decisions by companies, but there are several ways in which the base information can be presented to management so as to provide a better foundation upon which to take the decision.

Three-Level Estimates
In the production of any cash flow for an investment appraisal, those concerned will have had to make assumptions in several areas, for example:

    — the level of demand
    — the cost of materials
    — the price charged
    — the product life cycle
    — the capital required
    — the working capital required.

If a company were considering manufacturing and selling a product, it would have to consider all these factors, and many more, in preparing a cash flow. If they were to present a single cash flow proposal, as illustrated in this chapter, this would not contain the necessary information for those taking the decision to allocate capital. More is required for a good decision to be made.

One simple way to provide more information about the proposed investment is to produce three cash flows: one for the best conditions likely to prevail under the project, one for the worst conditions, and a third for the most likely outcome. These can then be set out as:

	Best	*Most likely*	*Worst*
Capital outlay			
Annual cash flow			

When these are discounted either for the rate of return or the net present value, they provide an overall feel for the project upon which management can base a decision. These are the assumptions as to the best and worst outcomes of the investment, and must be as realistic as possible in order for full benefit to be achieved from this method.

If it is seen that the return on the project can be between 25% and 8%, then management can set this against the cost of raisng the funds and see if it is feasible. If the cost of capital to the firm is 12%, then they can weigh the risk of the project only returning 8% in their decision. If the firm cannot afford under any circumstances a return of 8% from this investment it can be rejected as too risky for the firm to undertake even though there is a possibility of returns as high as 25%.

Sensitivity Analysis

A further means of improving the data upon which the investment decision is to be taken is to study the proposal to see which factors have the greatest impact on its success. This is known as sensitivity analysis. For example, if the investment is concerned with a new product, it may be found that the critical factor is the uncertainty of demand for the new product. In this case the investment proposal can be framed so as to highlight this fact, and show a series of cash flows and returns on the project at differing levels of demand. For example, the information may be as follows:

		Year 1	2	3	4	Total
Capital outlay		£100,000				£100,000
Demand (units)	(A)	300	500	300	100	1,200
	(B)	400	600	400	150	1,550
	(C)	500	800	800	200	2,300
	(D)	600	1,000	800	100	2,500

These represent different demand patterns that the product may achieve, and the cash flow for each demand pattern (in £'000) is:

	Year 1	2	3	4
Demand pattern (A)	30	50	30	10
(B)	40	55	40	10
(C)	55	85	90	20
(D)	70	120	90	15

The net present values of these cash flows when discounted at 10% are:

Demand pattern	(A)	(B)	(C)	(D)
Net present value discounted at 10%	(−£2,000)	£19,000	£101,000	£141,000
Rate of return	9%	20%	54%	73%

With this information management is in a better position to assess the proposal. Demand is the most sensitive factor in the eventual profitability of the project, and a range of different demand patterns that may be expected are shown together with their present values and returns.

This sort of analysis can also be used effectively where it is a machine installation that is being considered. Different life expectancies can be used to assess the viability of the investment — i.e. what happens to the return on the investment if the machine only lasts for two years rather than five.

Expected Value

It is also possible to incorporate simple statistical techniques into the investment proposal. One very useful technique is that of expected value. An example will illustrate its use:

	Demand	Cash flow	Probability	Expected value
Year 1	300 units	£30,000	0.3	£9,000
	400 units	40,000	0.4	16,000
	500 units	55,000	0.2	11,000
	600 units	70,000	0.1	7,000
			1.0	£43,000

The demand that is seen as being possible in the first year together with the cash flow that would result are set out in the table, and against each of these possible outcomes is a probability of occurrence. The sales manager is asked to place a probability on the likely occurrence of each demand level, and in this case he has estimated that there is a 30% chance of 300 units being demanded, 40% of 400, 20% of 500 and a 10% chance of 600 units. The probability of occurrence is multiplied by the outcome and the results totalled to provide the expected value. In this example the expected cash flow for the first year is £43,000.

This figure of £43,000 is more useful than a straighforward average which would show a value of:

$$\frac{£30,000 + £40,000 + £55,000 + £70,000}{4} = £48,750$$

as it takes into account the estimated likelihood of the event — in this case the cash flow for each level of demand. It is also better than just taking the most likely event — that is, the one which has the highest probability of occurrence — of £40,000, because it takes into account that there is a significant probability that it will either be more or less than this amount.

It is possible to calculate the expected cash flows for each year of a project's life, and use these in the discounting calculations. The resulting figures are better than the single cash flow estimates normally produced. The whole range of possible outcomes is covered, not just the average or most likely. So this method gives a better appreciation of the project's potential.

Monte Carlo Simulation

A further refinement which can be adopted in the presentation of investment proposals to enable those allocating the capital to have a better understanding of the likely outcomes is to apply probability analysis. As far as a practical application of probability analysis is concerned, it is necessary to have access to computer facilities. But the technique is outlined here because of its importance in understanding the methods of investment analysis nowadays. Even a small firm can obtain access to computer facilities. Indeed, any firm wishing to have an analysis on an investment decision may only need to contact the university or polytechnic in its locality to have assistance from a student (together with the institution's computer facilities) at low cost and to great advantage.

The first step in applying probability analysis to a proposal is to outline the key factors upon which eventual profitability depends. This is exactly what was done with sensitivity analysis as illustrated earlier in this chapter. With a new product decision these factors would mainly be concerned with cost, price and volume, and with a new labour-saving machine investment they might be capital cost, savings and machine life.

Having isolated these factors, probabilities are applied to their possible outcomes. For example, consider the following data on an investment proposal:

Working capital		Annual revenue		Annual running costs	
£'000	Prob. %	£'000	Prob. %	£'000	Prob. %
10–20	10	5–10	25	3–6	5
20–30	60	10–15	50	6–9	15
30–40	25	15–20	20	9–12	70
40–50	5	20–25	5	12–15	10

This can be graphed either as a cumulative probability curve

then these can be used for the three factors as follows:

		Capital outlay	Annual revenue	Annual running costs
Random choice	(A)	20 = £22,000	74 = £14,000	94 = £13,500
	(B)	22 = £23,000	15 = £6,000	93 = £13,000
	(C)	45 = £26,000	44 = £12,000	16 = £8,000
	(D)	04 = £14,000	32 = £10,500	03 = £4,500

The monetary values are found from the cumulative probability graph and shown by the dotted lines. Each one of the combinations will provide a different present value and rate of return, and if sufficient random samples are taken, a comprehensive picture of the likely outcomes of the investment will be available. This can be used by management to decide whether or not to accept the proposal and allocate capital to its initiation.

It is also possible to use the frequency distribution in the same manner. In the sampling method one provides for the choice to be weighted by the probability of its occurrence. Thus, for example, there would be more use made of the running costs between £9,000 and £12,000 than of any other level because these have the highest probability of occurring.

The use of probability analysis does not solve the problem of the investment decision for management. It merely provides better information or insight into the possible outcomes, or the ranges of potential profitability, of the project. The manager must still do what he is paid for, and that is to apply his knowledge, experience and ability to the best solution. There is as yet no substitute for this.

7 Introduction to Management Accounting

It is often thought that costing systems exist so as to provide a basis for adequate pricing decisions. Calculating the cost of a product is certainly important in setting effective prices, but this is by no means its only use. The main purpose of a costing system is to enable management to control operations, and to plan for future growth and profitability. Cost accounting has a very wide application in all aspects of management. A firm cannot be effectively run without some idea of what costs are incurred and if the various elements of cost and their behaviour are not understood and monitored. Planning cannot be undertaken without knowledge of how the various costs will react to changes in the level of operations, and how they will affect profitability. The simple formula:

$$\text{Profit} = \text{Revenue} - \text{Costs}$$

highlights the importance of cost. Costing systems are designed to give management the ability to control their costs and to understand how the various costs of their operations react to changes in volume or in relation to other factors. This chapter commences with a study of the different types of cost, and then goes on to consider various costing systems.

7.1. Types of Cost

There are many ways of classifying costs, and many different bits of terminology to describe those costs. This chapter and Chapter 8 use, as far as possible, common and simple terms in outlining cost behaviour and cost systems. Every manager is firmly recommended to visit the management accountant in his firm and discover what methods of costing are used and what terminology is adopted. The accountant will be glad to explain both terminology and method to an interested manager. If he is not, then it is possible the firm is employing the wrong management accountant. The management accountant is employed to provide management with information for decision-making. If managers cannot understand the methods used to provide the information, then the system is of little benefit, and the accountant is failing to communicate with those he is intended to service.

One basic classification of cost that the accountant must make is in relation to the time scale of the expenditure. If an expenditure is made in the current financial year, but will have continued benefits in future years, then it may be spread over a number of years as a charge in the Profit and Loss Account. The expenditure has been 'capitalised'. Thus, if a machine is purchased in one year, but is expected to have a life of at least five years, then the accountant may spread the expense over five years' accounts. The total amount of expenditure is capitalised and written off over a number of years. This need not apply only to physical assets, but could also be used for such expenditures as advertising and research and development where the benefits of current expenditure will accrue in future periods.

If an item is not capitalised, then it will be treated as a revenue expense or an income charge. That is, it will be written off in the accounts for the year in which it was incurred. For example, routine maintenance to keep the firm's machinery working efficiently will tend to be written off in the year in which it is undertaken.

The manner in which various expenditures are treated as either capital or revenue is important in that the decision will have a direct impact on the profit shown in the firm's accounts. This was shown in the earlier chapters of this book dealing with financial reports. There is rarely only one correct approach to the decision, and much will rely on the current practice in the firm concerned. In major companies changes will be noticed and commented upon by the financial analysts, e.g. Rolls-Royce and their research and development expenditures.

Having decided in which year the expense belongs, one can then move to a consideration of the elements of costs. These can be illustrated as follows:

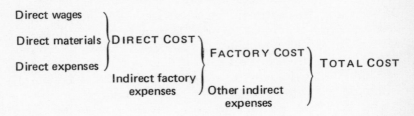

The accountant should all the time be endeavouring to provide management with a realistic cost upon which to base current control activities and budgets for future profitability. But there has yet to be devised a single correct way of calculating 'the cost' of a product. Each firm will have its own system of cost data. This diversity underlines the need for managers to discover from their own accountant which approach is used in their own firm. The problems of ascertaining a cost can be shown by taking each element of cost in turn.

The direct costs of a product are those costs which can be accurately and indisputably placed against units of output. Direct wages are wages paid to employees on the shop floor physically to produce the products being manufactured by a firm. It may be thought that with wages there will be no problems of discovering the true cost of production. There will be job cards to show which workers did what and when. But what about the problem of overtime or bonus payments? Does it mean that the customer who purchases products made whilst workers were on overtime must pay more for them? And how are PAYE, insurance, holiday pay and training to be treated? The accountant must estimate and make assumptions to provide management with the direct labour content and cost of units of output. There is no readily available and indisputable direct wage cost.

Direct materials are those materials that are used in the production of the products of the firm. But, as was illustrated in Chapter 2, there are many methods of valuing materials and charging them out to production. It will depend whether LIFO, FIFO, average cost or some other method of stock valuation is adopted as to what figure will be placed on the direct materials used in producing the products. The figure that is shown in the manufacturing account of the firm for materials used in production is developed from certain basic assumptions and estimates made by the accountant, and in order to make use of the accountant's information the manager must understand what these are.

Together with the direct expenses associated with the physical production of the goods to be sold there are other indirect expenses. These are expenses that cannot with accuracy be assigned to units of output. They will consist of such items as management salaries, insurance, rates, interest on loans, depreciation and research.

Indirect expenses cannot be accurately assigned to production and sale of products and so must be allocated in some manner by the accountant. Whilst there are many accepted methods of allocation, there is no single agreed method that can be used to provide 'the' correct cost data on a product. For example, any one of the various methods of depreciation outlined in Chapter 2 could be applied, and each would tend to provide a different loading of indirect cost to units of output, but none could be said to be incorrect. It is a matter of judgement and opinion by the accountant. In order to discover the cost of a department or section in a works, it will be necessary for there to be rule-of-thumb allocations of overall indirect expenses. These allocation methods will be discussed later in this chapter, and some of the problems associated with them dealt with in Chapter 8.

It is possible to split the various costs of a business into two major parts — the variable costs and the fixed costs. Variable costs are those costs which change in direct proportion to output. For example, the direct material and wages can be taken as being variable costs in that if the material content of a product is £10 and the labour necessary to assemble and pack it is £20, then for each unit there will be a cost of £30. If 100 units are produced the cost will be £3,000, if 400 are produced, £12,000, and so on. The cost varies in direct proportion to the number produced. A fixed cost is one which does not change in relation to variations in output or sales. The rent and rates of a factory will remain constant whatever the level of output achieved up to the point where a new factory is built or an extension added to the existing one to cater for the increased volume.

It is possible to graph these costs as illustrated below:

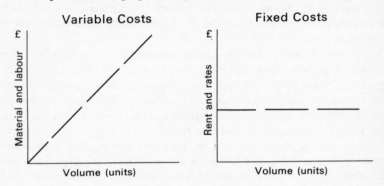

and to combine them into a graph showing the total cost (assuming there are no other expenses) at various levels of volume:

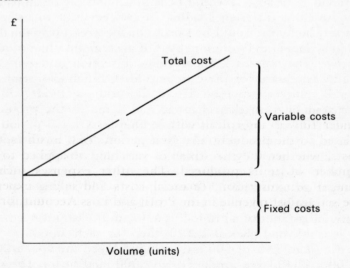

This approach will be further developed in Chapter 8, which discusses break-even analysis and marginal costing.

Clearly, in any firm there will be many costs which cannot neatly be split into a variable and a fixed element, and assumptions will have to be made as to how costs behave, but this does not invalidate the approach for analysis of business situations. In many firms labour cannot be taken as a truly variable cost as the firm must keep its skilled employees on the payroll even if for short periods there is little for them to do. It cannot be assumed that skilled labour can be hired and fired as production fluctuations dictate, and so labour may be treated as, at least in part, a fixed cost.

One final classification of costs is the differentiation between product costs and period costs. Product costs are those that relate to the production of the goods being sold by the firm, and will consist of all costs incurred in producing the goods to be sold. Thus, product costs will include all direct costs, such as labour and materials, and all other costs and expenses that can be directly related to the production of goods in the firm. Period costs are costs which relate to a particular time of period rather than to the physical production of units. These costs will be set against the revenue generated in the period in which they are incurred, and not allocated to units of production. It will depend upon which type of costing system is adopted by a firm as to which costs are classified as period costs rather than product costs. The more common types of costing systems are described in the following sections of this chapter.

7.2. Full or Absorption Costing

Under full or absorption costing the costs for a period are related to the production of that period. That is, all factory costs, whether they are fixed or variable, are applied to the number of units produced. The other expenses such as general administration, financial costs and selling expenses are set against revenue in the Profit and Loss Account for the period, but are not allocated to units of production.

This method of costing provides a stock valuation at 'full cost'. Indirect expenses are included in the stock valuation. Whilst full costing is still widely used in industry, there are several problems connected with its application, and these are illustrated in the introduction to marginal costing in Chapter

8. However, the major difficulties can be said to be:

(i) In concentrating on factory costs, full costing ignores major expenses of the firm such as selling, distribution, financial and administration.

(ii) As a result of (i) above, management often has to use gross profit margins rather than net profit margin, particularly in the pricing decision. This can be misleading in effective pricing.

(iii) As the cost of a unit of production is found by dividing the total factory cost by the number of units produced, there is no firm cost for management to use. As volume changes, so will the 'cost' per unit.

(iv) Following from (iii) above, full costing is of little benefit to management in forward planning of profitable growth.

(v) As a result of using full costing it is possible for management to reject profitable opportunities to use spare capacity. (See Chapter 8 for a detailed explanation to this.)

7.3. Overhead Application

In any firm there will be a major section of costs that cannot with accuracy be assigned to products or departments. These are the indirect costs or overheads. The accountant is expected to provide cost details that include the indirect costs, and he must therefore use some method to spread or apply these overheads. There are many such methods, but only the most common ones are illustrated here.

The simplest method is to take the total overhead figure and divide it by the number of units produced. But this is not often acceptable, as it assumes each unit is identical and should share equally in the indirect costs, and in a situation where a company is manufacturing many products this is unlikely to be the case.

A very common method is to apply the overheads in relation to the direct labour hours or cost for the various products or units produced. Where labour is the critical factor in the operation, then this is a useful basis for applying overheads. The rate can be calculated as follows:

$$\frac{\text{Estimated overhead}}{\text{Estimated direct labour cost for period}}$$

or

$$\frac{\text{Estimated overhead}}{\text{Estimated direct labour hours for period}}$$

The rate of application that is produced is then used in relation to whichever denominator has been used in the equation. When labour cost is used as the denominator, then there may be problems where employees on different pay scales do the same work. For instance, if overheads are recovered on the basis of 100% on labour cost, then a skilled man at £4 per hour will incur £4 per hour indirect costs on the job in which he is involved, but an unskilled man at £2 per hour doing the same job, perhaps producing one unit of output, will have only £2 indirect cost to be applied.

It is also possible to calculate machine hour rates to charge overheads to production. In this case the equation becomes:

$$\frac{\text{Estimated overhead}}{\text{Estimated machine hours}}$$

This method is particularly applicable in machine shops, where different rates will be calculated for each machine or group of machines. However, there will be difficulties in calculating the machine hour rates and also in keeping records of machine hours worked on individual jobs or units, and thus application on the basis of labour tends to be the more common method, since it is simpler to operate.

7.4. Standard Costing

Standard costing has long been seen as a useful way of providing effective control of operations, that is, to estimate what costs should be under normal operating efficiency. With some predetermined standard in mind it is much easier to control actual operation costs. It can quickly be made evident where problems are arising and which manager or department is responsible. Actual costs are compared against the standards and the resulting variances are analysed to show which factor has produced the variance. If the actual costs are higher than the standard, then this can be the result of price rises which make the item being used more expensive, or because more of it has been used than was expected.

Standards may be set for all elements of cost — material, labour and overheads — and of varying degrees of rigour. For example, the standard that is set may be one based on historic experience and may not change from period to period. This is not a particularly challenging standard, but one that does provide a common base for performance and efficiency measurement. However, as this standard may soon become out of date, it is not of real practical use in cost control. At the other extreme it is possible to set an ideal standard, that is, a standard that can only possibly be attained if everything works perfectly and there are no problems. If management sees such a challenging standard as likely to produce more effort from their employees, then it may be of use, but it can result in these standards being disregarded as completely beyond the reach of anyone. Another method is to define a standard which can be attained with normal operating efficiency and effort, that is, a standard that is lower than the ideal but which will require an effort to achieve. It is this last standard that is normally used in business. The employees are given a standard which they can attain with full effort, and one which will be useful in comparing actual performance with expected results. The motivational implications of standards are discussed in Chapter 9, which deals with budgetary control.

In defining standards for materials it is essential that those concerned be involved. It is not normally possible for the accountant to do this by himself. The main person or department concerned will be the purchasing manager or department, and they will be called to account for at least part of any variances between actual and standard materials costs. The standard will be based on an estimate of material prices in the coming period, and actual prices compared with these standards to assess the efficiency of purchasing and also the accuracy and currency of the standard.

The standard cost of materials will also depend upon the amount that it is expected will be used during the period, and it will be necessary to split the overall material cost variance into its two component parts, price and use. A price variance and a usage variance will be shown as is illustrated in the example below:

To produce 100 units of a product, the standard cost of material is £2,000, the standard amount of materials being 1,000 lb and the standard price being £2. The actual cost of producing 100 units was found to be £2,640 in using 1,200 lb of material at a cost of £2.2.

Standard cost = 1,000 lb at £2 =	£2,000
Actual cost = 1,200 lb at £2.2 =	£2,640
Total adverse variance	£640

Price variance
Actual quantity of materials multiplied by price difference
(1,200)   x   (£2 − £2.2)   = £240

Usage variance
Standard price multiplied by usage difference
(£2)   x   (1,000 − 1,200)   = £400
                                                               £640

The price variance is found by taking the actual quantity of materials purchased and using the difference between the actual price paid and the standard set to calculate the amount of the overall variance that can be shown to be due to price change in the material used. This variance can be used by the purchasing department to measure their efficiency in getting the lowest price for materials required.

The usage variance is found by taking the standard price and the difference between the actual quantity used and the standard set. This variance could be used by the factory manager to assess the efficiency of his production.

Exactly the same procedure would be followed for analysing labour variances. There would be a standard payment rate for the work and a standard time allotted for its completion. The overall variance can then be split into the price, or rate, variance and the usage or efficiency variance. An example is provided below:

The standard for a unit is 10 hours at £2 per hour = £20
The actual for a unit was 9 hours at £2.5 per hour = £22.5

£2.5

Rate variance
Actual hours multiplied by rate difference
    (9)   ×   (£2 − £2.5)   = £4.5

Efficiency variance
Standard rate multiplied by time difference
    (£2)   ×   (10 − 9)   = £2.0

£2.5

These two variances may then be given to those responsible for the activities. The manager who is responsible for efficient working can see that although he produced one unit for fewer hours, the rate of pay was excessive; this can also be shown to the manager in charge of rates of pay. Control action can be taken as necessary.

These types of variance can be illustrated in the form of a diagram:

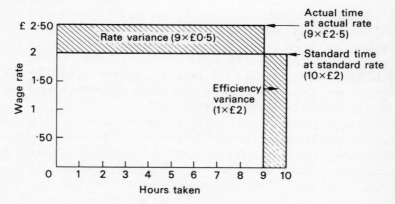

From this diagram can be clearly seen the favourable variance of completing the work in one hour better than standard, and the adverse variance of paying more than the standard rate for those nine hours' work. Had the actual time taken been 11 hours, then the diagram would have appeared as:

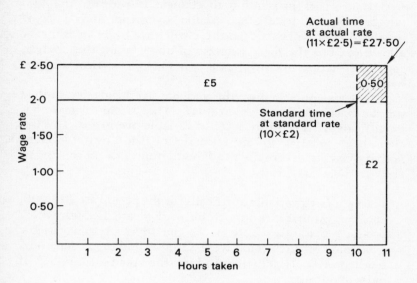

It can be seen that the right-hand corner square could be taken in either of the two variances. It could either be taken as part of the rate variance to make this £5.50, or in the efficiency variance to make this £2.50. It is normally the convention that it appear as part of the rate variance, but there is always that area of dispute when fixing responsibility for the adverse variance.

In setting overhead standards it is necessary to define some level of activity upon which to base the rate of applying the overheads. Management requires similar information concerning overheads to that used with labour and materials. Is the variance due to the fact that more than expected was spent, or due to a different level of activity than was used in setting the standard? Where overheads represent a significant proportion of costs in an operation, it is important that they be controlled and monitored just as regularly as the direct costs. The method by which the overheads are applied may be either on the basis of labour, materials or machine hours, and upon the basis of an estimate of the activity to be experienced in the coming period. To allow full benefit from standard costing it is necessary to split overheads into the part that varies in relation to changes in output, and that which remains fixed — a variable overhead and a fixed overhead component. Often there will have to be an arbitrary allocation, but the mere exercise of undertaking this analysis into the nature of overhead expenses in a firm can be beneficial.

In the example below, the variable overheads are applied on the basis of direct labour-hours. That is, an estimate has been made of the future level of variable overheads. This has then been related to an estimate of the future level of activity, so as to obtain the labour hour rate necessary to recover those overheads:

The estimated variable overheads for the period are £25,000, and the estimated hours to be worked are 12,500, which produce a standard rate of £2 per hour. Actual variable overheads for the period were £33,000 and the actual hours worked were 15,000 to produce the standard number of units of output.

Spending variance

(The actual variable overhead rate is

$$\frac{£33,000}{15,000} = £2.2 \text{ per hour})$$

Actual hours worked multiplied by rate difference

(15,000)	x	(£2 − £2.2) =	£3,000

Efficiency variance
Standard rate multiplied by hours difference

(£2)	x	(12,500 − 15,000) =	£5,000
			£8,000

Check

Actual variable overhead	£33,000
Standard variable overhead	£25,000
Overall variance	£8,000

Here the variance between the actual and the standard amount of variable overheads is found by subtracting the actual overhead rate (£2.2 per hour) from the standard rate and multiplying by the actual hours worked. The procedure is similar for all variance analysis. The efficiency variance here is calculated in the same manner as for the labour efficiency variance. The actual and standard hours worked are related to the standard hourly rate (£2). These variances show how the overall adverse variance of £8,000 is divided between overspending and exceeding standard hours worked in production. Once again, the relevant variances should be investigated by those with responsibility in that area.

The final variances to be mentioned are those of fixed overheads. The fixed overheads of a firm are likely to remain constant despite fluctuations in volume around a normal level of activity. If a unit cost is required, then clearly the higher the volume of output the lower the amount each unit should bear of overall fixed costs, and thus the lower the unit cost. The accountant is faced with the task of presenting an acceptable standard cost that can be used by management, despite monthly variations in volume. So it is necessary to decide upon some 'normal' level of activity to provide a rate at which the fixed overheads are applied to units of output.

Which level of activity to use in setting the standard is a matter of judgement by management and the accountant. One level of 'normal' activity might be that which the factory is expected to average over the next few years; or the estimated level of activity for the coming year may be used.

The chosen level of activity is then used to produce an overhead rate. Thus, if the fixed overheads for the period are estimated to be £20,000 and the direct labour hours 10,000, then a rate of £2 per direct labour hour can be used. Otherwise the £20,000 may be related to any other element that is considered effective in applying fixed overheads. If the firm works only 9,000 hours but incurs fixed overheads of £25,000, the variances may be calculated as follows:

Standard fixed overheads £20,000; actual £25,000
Standard hours to be worked 10,000; actual 9,000

Actual fixed overhead applied (9,000 x £2)	= £18,000
Actual fixed overheads incurred	= £25,000
Overall variance	£7,000

Expenditure variance
Standard overheads less actual overheads

(£20,000)	—	(£25,000)	= £5,000

Volume variance
Standard rate multiplied by hours difference

(£2)	x	(10,000 − 9,000)	= £2,000
			£7,000

These variances show the impact of fixed overheads exceeding the standard and of the number of hours worked falling below standard. They combine to explain the overall actual variance of £7,000.

It is possible to develop variance analysis further to show an efficiency variance and a capacity variance for the fixed overheads. The efficiency variance shows the gain or loss from the actual output being below or above the standard time allowed, and the capacity variance deals with the change in the unit overhead cost due to changes in the level of activity.

7.5. Interpretation of Variances

The first thing is to warn the manager to discover what variances are calculated in his firm under standard costing and also, most important, how they are calculated. The above examples show in broad outline the type of variance analysis that can be undertaken, but every firm has its own methods and terminology. If the outline has been understood, then this can be related to the individual firm.

It must not be assumed that all standard costing systems will use the same basis as the examples shown above. Not only may the method of calculation be different, but also the method of presentation. It is quite usual to see the standard costing variances expressed in ratio or percentage terms. For example, the labour rate variance may be shown as:

$$\frac{\text{Actual hours at actual rate}}{\text{Actual hours at standard rate}} \times 100 = \%$$

The presentation of variances in management reports does not of itself ensure better control of costs. Control can only be achieved by in-depth investigation of the causes of the variances. In such a study it is often useful to separate those variances that are beyond the control of management from those which clearly are controllable. For example, if all suppliers of the firm's raw materials have increased their prices by 10%, then there is little point is spending a lot of time investigating the materials price variance that arises from this fact; it is beyond the control of the purchasing department — though they might try to get the product redesigned, or look for a substitute.

Management must also decide what size of variance is worth attention. If every variance is investigated fully, then this will waste time and possibly bring the whole control system to a halt by annoying the managers concerned. Some level has to be set at which a study will be undertaken to see why the variance arose and what should be done about it. What this level is will depend upon the type of firm and its size. For example, a level of ±10% could be set, or all variances over £500, beyond which a full investigation will be made and those responsible be called to explain.

Standard costing variances seldom provide the answer to questions. They merely show that questions should be asked. But standard costing systems provide a basis for sound and speedy control. Problem areas are quickly pinpointed, so that management can take the necessary action before it is too late. Standard costing also enables each key manager to see what impact his function has on the overall success of the firm. It also enables regular reports on each part of his responsibility comparing standard with actual performance.

7.6. Process Costing

Where the firm is producing a continuous flow of product which moves from one process to another through the factory, rather than individual units of a product, process costing is used. Process costing follows the progress of the product from its introduction into the production system through the various processes and into its saleable form. It is used in process industries such as chemicals, textiles and foods. The intention is to discover the cost of the product at each stage in the overall production process so as to show productive efficiency, spoilage and waste. It should provide management with sufficient information to take any necessary control action.

To operate process costing, the factory is divided into separate departments or processes. Each of these departments is responsible for one particular activity. For example, in a textile firm one department may card, one dye, one spin, and one weave the cloth. Each department has its own costs identified — material, labour and indirect expenses — and these are recorded against production as the product moves to the next stage in the process. Quite often standards are set for each department, so allowing the use of standard costing in the process flow. The finished stock of one process moves to become the raw material of the next until the product is ready for sale to customers.

Under process costing, great attention is paid to the loss, scrap, spoil and general wastage that is experienced. Normal losses can be estimated and abnormal loss highlighted to management for necessary action.

With continuous flow production there is a problem when it is necessary to discover the work-in-progress level for accounting purposes. How should the work in the process be valued? One widely used method is to calculate the equivalent production and allocate costs on this basis. The equivalent production is found by studying the process to see how far towards completion are the units. If 1,000 units are 50% completed, then this is taken to be the same as 500 units fully complete.

In process costing, joint products often arise, that is, two or more products are produced from the same process. In

these circumstances it is necessary for the accountant to
estimate upon some acceptable basis the division of cost
between these products. There may also be by-products,
produced incidentally as the main products are processed.
Again, some estimate of the cost to be set against these
by-products will have to be made by the accountant.

7.7. Contract Costing
Contract costing is the opposite in many ways to process
costing. With contract costing each contract or job has its
own account, and costs are collected against this. This form
of costing is particularly applicable to civil engineering and
construction work, but also widely used in heavy engineering — ships, large transformers, etc.

Each job or contract is assigned an accounts code or
number and all work done on that contract is charged against
that code. All materials issued from stores or specially
purchased bear the number of the contract; all labour and,
where possible, all indirect costs are also set against the
particular contract.

By recording all costs associated with a particular contract
in this manner, management can have a continuous flow of
information by which to monitor progress against planned
performance, and also to see what profit has been returned
on each contract.

8 Contribution Analysis

In the previous chapter various types of costing systems were examined to see how they assisted in the definition and control of a firm's costs. In this chapter the concept of marginal costing is explained, and its use illustrated. For it enables information to be presented in a simple and readily understandable form, for management decisions in such areas as pricing and make-or-buy situations.

8.1. The Problem of Overhead Allocation

If a firm had drafted the budgets for the coming year, they might appear as:

Budgeted sales:	1,000 units at a price of £22		£22,000
Budgeted direct costs:			
Materials	£5,000		
Labour	£4,000		
Other	£3,000		£12,000
Budgeted indirect costs:			
Administration expenses		£4,000	
Financial charges (depreciation, etc)		£3,000	£7,000
			£19,000

Cost per unit (£19,000/1,000) = £19
Profit per unit (£22 − £19) = £3
Budgeted profit for year (£3 x 1,000) = £3,000

The company expects to make £3 profit per unit as the difference between the full cost per unit (as defined under absorption costing in Chapter 7) and the selling price of £22, and produce £3,000 overall profit for the year at the budgeted level of sales.

If the company had prepared budgets for an output and

148

sale of 800 units of the product, then the figures would have been:

Sales income: 800 units at a price of £22		£17,600
Budgeted direct costs:		
Materials	£4,000	
Labour	£3,200	
Other	£2,400	£9,600
Budgeted indirect costs:		
Administration	£4,000	
Financial	£3,000	£7,000
		£16,600

Cost per unit (£16,600/800) = £20.75
Profit per unit (£22 − £22.75) = £1.25
Budgeted profit for the year = £1,000

However, the company may have originally budgeted to produce and sell 800 units of its product and then actually achieved production and sales of 1,000 units during the year. If they wish to calculate the profitability before a set of annual accounts are prepared, they might do the following calculation:

Budgeted profit per unit (£1.25) x 1,000 units sold
= Profit of £1,250

So the profit for the year appears to be £1,250. But on the previous page where a budget was done for 1,000 units a profit of £3,000 was shown. There are now two different, and substantially different, profit figures for making and selling 1,000 units of the product. Which is correct, the £1,250 or the £3,000?

Clearly, it must be the £3,000 which comes from the budget to produce and sell 1,000 units of the product. These figures relate to production and sale of 1,000 units, so if all goes according to plan, the profit made will be £3,000, not £1,250.

The reason for the differences in the two profit figures is the indirect costs. These are assumed to be fixed in so far as it does not matter whether the company produces 800 or 1,000 units; they will remain the same. The administration salaries, rent and rates, etc., will still be £4,000 and the financial charges will still be £3,000 at 800 units output and sale.

When the company calculated the cost per unit at 800 units output and sale it assumed that each unit would bear 1/800th of the £7,000 indirect costs, or £8.75 per unit. Yet when the company actually achieves output and sale of 1,000 units, each unit should bear only 1/1000th of the £7,000, or £7 per unit.

Thus, in taking the £8.75 per unit indirect cost allocation into the calculations, each unit is having to bear £1.75 too much indirect costs (£8.75 − £7). If this £1.75 is multiplied by the 1,000 units it provides the £1,750 difference between the £1,250 and the £3,000 profits.

The company using the 800 unit budget data has been overcharging each unit for the recovery of its total indirect expenses. It has been over-recovering the indirect expenses, and this might be shown on the accountant's report as:

Profit from sale of 1,000 units	£1,250
Over-recovery of indirect expenses	£1,750
Profit for the year	£3,000

It will always be found that where a company is using full or absorption costing to provide a unit cost and profit figure, there will be an overstatement of real profitability if the budget output is not attained, and an understatement of profit when it is exceeded. Indirect expenses will have been under- or over-recovered, and allowance must be made for this in assessing real profitability.

As a further example of problems that can be created by the allocation of indirect or overhead expenses and costs to units of output, the following dialogue is reprinted from the *Lybrand Journal*:

In discussing the costs incident to various types of operations, the analogy was drawn of the Restaurant which adds a rack of peanuts to the counter, intending to pick up a little additional profit in the usual course of business. This analogy was attacked as an over-simplification. However, the accuracy of the analogy is evident when one considers the actual problem faced by the Restauranteur (Joe) as revealed by his Accountant-Efficiency-Expert:

EFF EX: Joe, you said you put in these peanuts because some people ask for them, but do you realise what this rack of peanuts is *costing* you?

JOE: It ain't gonna cost. 'Sgonna be a profit. Sure I hadda pay $25 for a fancy rack to holda bags, but the peanuts cost 6c a bag but I sell 'em for 10c. Figger I sell 50 bags a week to start. It'll take 12½ weeks to cover the cost of the rack. After that I gotta clear profit of 4c a bag. The more I sell, the more I make.

EFF EX: That is an antiquated and completely unrealistic approach, Joe. Fortunately, modern accounting procedures permit a more accurate picture which reveals the complexities involved.

JOE: Huh?

EFF EX: To be precise, Those peanuts must be integrated into your entire operation and be allocated their appropriate share of business overhead. They must share a proportionate part of your expenditures for rent, heat, light, equipment depreciation, decorating, salaries for your waitresses, cook. . . .

JOE: The *cook*? What's a he gotta do wit'a peanuts? He don' even know I got 'em!

EFF EX: Look Joe, the cook is in the kitchen, the kitchen prepares the food, the food is what brings people in here, and the people ask to buy peanuts. *That's* why you must charge a portion of the cook's wages, as well as a part of your own salary, to peanut sales. This sheet contains a carefully calculated cost analysis which indicates the peanut operation should pay exactly $1,278 per year toward these general overhead costs.

JOE: The peanuts? $1,278 a year for overhead? The Nuts?

EFF EX: It's really a little more than that. You also spend money each week to have the windows washed, to have the place swept out in the mornings, keep soap in the washroom and provide free cokes to the police. That raises the total to $1,313 per year.

JOE (*Thoughtfully*): But the peanut salesman said I'd make money . . . put 'em on the end of the counter, he said . . . and get 4c a bag profit. . . .

EFF EX (*With a sniff*): He's not an accountant. Do you actually know what the portion of the counter occupied by the peanut rack is worth to you?

JOE: Ain't worth nothing — no stool there . . . just a dead spot at the end.

EFF EX: The modern cost picture permits no dead spots. Your counter contains 60 square feet and your counter business grosses $15,000 a year. Consequently, the square foot of space occupied by the peanut rack is worth $250 per year. Since you have taken that area away from general counter use, you must charge the value of the space to the occupant.

JOE: You mean I gotta add *$250 a year more* to the *peanuts*?

EFF EX: Right. That raises their share of the general operating costs to a grand total of $1,563 per year. Now then, if you sell 50 bags of peanuts per week, these allocated costs will amount to 60c per bag.

JOE: WHAT?

EFF EX: Obviously, to that must be added your purchase price of 6c per bag, which brings the total to 66c. So you see by selling peanuts at 10c per bag, you are losing 56c on every sale.

JOE: Somethin's crazy!

EFF EX: Not at all! Here are the *figures*. They prove your peanuts operation cannot stand on its own feet.

JOE (*Brightening*): Suppose I sell *lotsa* peanuts . . . thousand bags a week 'stead of fifty.

EFF EX (*Tolerantly*): Joe, you don't understand the problem. If the volume of peanut sales increases our operating costs will go up . . . you'll have to handle more bags with more time, more depreciation, more everything. The basic principle of accounting is firm on that subject. 'The Bigger the Operation the More

General Overhead Costs that must be Allocated'. No, increasing the volume of sales won't help.

JOE: Okay, You so smart, *you* tell *me* what I gotta do.

EFF EX (*Condescendingly*): Well ... you could first reduce operating expenses.

JOE: How?

EFF EX: Move to a building with cheaper rent. Cut salaries. Wash the windows bi-weekly. Have the floor swept only on Thurday. Remove the soap from the washrooms. Decrease the square foot value of your counter. For example, if you can cut your expenses 50%, that will reduce the amount allocated to peanuts from $1,563 to $781.50 per year, reducing the cost to 36c per bag.

JOE (*Slowly*): That's better?

EFF EX: Much, much better. However, even then you would lose 26c per bag if you only charge 10c. Therefore, you must also raise your selling price. If you want a net profit of 4c per bag you would have to charge 40c.

JOE (*Flabbergasted*): You mean even after I cut operating costs 50% I still gotta charge 40c for a 10c bag of peanuts? Nobody's that nuts about nuts! Who'd buy 'em?

EFF EX: That's a secondary consideration. The point is, at 40c you'd be selling at a price based upon a true and proper evaluation of your then reduced costs.

JOE (*Eagerly*): Look! I gotta better idea. Why don't I just throw the nuts out ... put 'em in a ash can?

EFF EX: Can you afford it?

JOE: Sure. All I got is about 50 bags of peanuts ... cost about three bucks ... so I lose $25 on the rack, but I'm outa this nutsy business and no more grief.

EFF EX (*Shaking head*): Joe, it isn't that simple. You are *in* the peanut business: The minute you throw those peanuts out you are adding $1,563 of annual overhead to the rest of your operation. Joe ... be realistic ... *can you afford to do that*?

JOE (*Completely crushed*): It's a unbelievable! Last week I was a make money. Now I'm in a trouble ... just

because I think peanuts on a counter is a gonna bring
me some extra profit ... just because I believe 50 bags
of peanuts a week is a easy.

EFF EX (*With raised eyebrows*): That is the object of
modern cost studies, Joe ... to dispel those false
illusions.

This last example illustrates the sort of arguments that so
upset several engineers towards the end of the last century
that they devoted their efforts to seeing how a more
satisfactory approach could be developed. The result of this
work provided the basis for modern cost—volume—profit
analysis. It is perhaps salutary for accountants to remember
that it is their profession that created the problem but not
the solution to overhead allocation.

Before considering the possible alternative means of
presenting information on costs of output, it is necessary to
take an apparent side-track into one aspect of cost—volume—
profit analysis: that of break-even analysis. The reasons for
this move will be evident later.

8.2. The Break-Even Point

R. H. Parker in his book *Management Accounting: An
Historical Perspective* (Macmillan, 1969) describes how the
first article on break-even charts appeared in the American
Engineering Magazine in December 1903. At this time the
manner in which costs behave — some remaining constant,
and some varying in direct proportion to output — was set
out, and the point at which total revenue exactly equalled
total cost was defined as the break-even point, the point at
which the firm made zero profit. At outputs above the
break-even point the firm will make a profit as revenue
exceeds cost, and below break-even output there will be a
loss as revenue is less than cost. These facts can be shown in a
traditional break-even chart.

To provide the basis for drawing a break-even chart, the
case of a man renting a stall in an antique market is taken. The
rent he has to pay for the stall is £30 for the day of the

market, and he has several framed prints which he has bought on sale or return from a supplier. These prints cost him £4 each and he is going to sell them for £10.

This information can be put into a break-even chart as illustrated below:

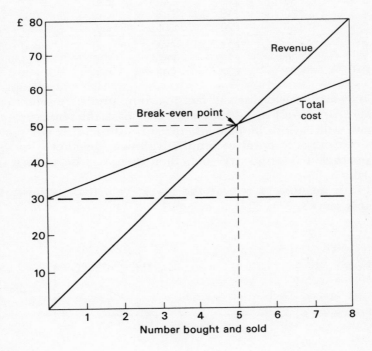

This chart shows the total cost and revenue for various levels of sales, and it can be seen that there is a break-even point at 5 units of sale. At this point the total cost exactly equals the total revenue. The total cost is built up of two component parts: the fixed cost of £30, that is, the rental that is to be paid for the stall, which remains constant however many prints are sold; and the variable cost of £4 per print.

It is possible to produce a matrix of these data in the following form:

Number bought and sold	Fixed cost	Variable cost	Total cost	Revenue	Profit/ loss
0	£30	£0	£30	£0	£–30
1	£30	£4	£34	£10	£–24
2	£30	£8	£38	£20	£–18
3	£30	£12	£42	£30	£–12
4	£30	£16	£46	£40	£–6
5	£30	£20	£50	£50	£0
6	£30	£24	£54	£60	£+6
7	£30	£28	£58	£70	£+12
8	£30	£32	£62	£80	£+18

This matrix highlights the fact that if no prints are sold, then there will be a loss of £30. The fixed cost, the rental for the stall, will have to be paid whether or not there are any sales. The break-even point of 5 units is shown, together with the fact that if 8 prints are sold, then there will be a profit of £18.

It is possible to redraft the break-even chart to illustrate these facts.

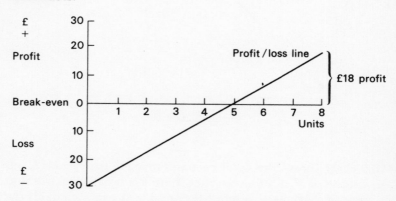

This type of chart is called a profit/volume chart, and uses a single line to represent the three lines in the traditional break-even chart. It is possible to read off the profit or loss for any given volume of output and sale without having to measure the distance between the cost line and revenue line on the break-even chart.

If it were necessary to draw a break-even or profit/volume

chart each time it was required to discover the break-even point of operations, this would be a rather time-consuming exercise, and so there is, needless to say, a formula by which the calculation can be done.

It has been stated that the break-even point is the level of output and sale at which the total costs exactly equal the total revenue, at which point zero profit is made.

Zero profit is where ⟶ Total cost = Total revenue

The two sides of this simple equation can be divided into their component parts:

Total revenue = Price multiplied by the number of units sold

Total cost = Fixed costs + (Variable cost multiplied by the number of units sold)

Thus, to find the break-even point it is necessary to find how many units have to be made and sold to complete the equation:

$$\text{Price} \times \text{Number of units}$$
$$\downarrow \qquad\qquad \downarrow$$
$$a \qquad\qquad x$$

$$= \text{Fixed cost} + (\text{Variable cost} \times \text{Number of units})$$
$$\downarrow \qquad\qquad \downarrow \qquad\qquad \downarrow$$
$$= \quad b \quad + \quad c \quad\qquad x$$

Giving each factor an algebraic symbol, the equation now becomes:

$$ax = b + cx$$

Solving this for x, the result is:

$$x = \frac{b}{a - c}$$

Putting this back into words, the number of units to be made and sold to provide zero profit is found by the following calculation:

$$= \frac{\text{Total fixed cost}}{\text{Unit price} - \text{Unit variable cost}}$$

To illustrate that this formula works, the data on the stallholder can be used. It is known that the fixed costs were £30, the price was £10 and the variable cost (the cost to get each unit into a saleable condition) was £4.

$$\text{Number of units to be bought and sold to break even} = \frac{£30}{£10 - £4} = 5 \text{ units}$$

The formula works.

8.3. Problems with Break-Even Charts

Having looked at the traditional break-even chart it is necessary to describe why this is rarely used as a decision-making aid in real life. The break-even chart is an ideal visual aid, and can be used at meetings, particularly sales and marketing meetings, to great effect. However, there are so many assumptions built into the three lines which appear on the chart as to render it useless for management decision-making situations. These assumptions are:

(a) That the costs associated with producing the various levels of output are constant, and capable of being represented by straight lines.

(b) There is only one selling price — i.e. no discounts for large quantities or for most favoured customers — enabling revenue to be shown as a straight line.

(c) There is a constant level of efficiency in production.

(d) The fixed costs remain constant over the range of output considered.

(e) There are no significant changes in inventory levels.

(f) Cost and revenue are only affected by volume changes.

(g) Costs can accurately be estimated over all levels of output.

In the examples so far, there has only been one product made and sold. If, as is more common, there are several products made and sold, then there is a further assumption which makes the break-even chart inoperable as a decision-making tool.

(h) That there is a constant sales mix.

To produce a graph which included a variable discount structure in the sales revenue line would not be impossible, but certainly difficult. If the fixed costs change at a certain level of operations — perhaps more space has to be rented — then this can give rise to a second break-even point. This can be illustrated with the stall-holder and the sale of prints. If he can hire an assistant and increase the size of his stall for £18, it will double his sales potential, but also produce a second break-even point, as can be seen from the graph below:

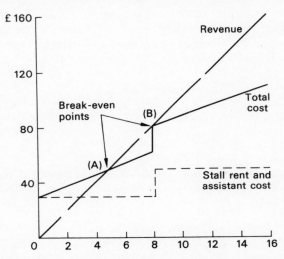

There are two points at which total revenue equals total costs. Five units and eight units bought and sold produce zero profit. Though this might at first be confusing for the stall-holder, it can provide a very useful basis upon which to assess his sales forecasts. If he considers that he will only sell about eight of the prints whatever he does, then he does not need more space and assistance, and can look for a profit maximum of £18. If, however, he feels with the increased space and assistance he can push sales up to 16 units, then it will be worthwhile to produce a profit of £48. The break-even chart has not provided any solutions; it has merely pointed out the key areas for further discussion and study. This is at best what any chart can do.

8.4. Contribution Analysis
Having shown that a break-even chart is not of real benefit in the decision-making process because of the limitations imposed by the assumptions that are made in its drafting, it is

now possible to consider the manner in which the break-even formula can be used.

The formula for finding the break-even point is:

$$\text{Number of units for break-even} = \frac{\text{Total fixed costs}}{\text{Unit price} - \text{Unit variable cost}}$$

Using the example from the beginning of this chapter (p. 148), if the direct or variable costs — that is, costs that vary in proportion to changes in volume of output — are set out, they appear as:

Materials	£5
Labour	4
Other	3
	£12 per unit

Given that the fixed costs are £7,000, it is a simple task using the break-even formula to calculate the number of units to be made and sold to break even:

$$\frac{£7,000}{£22 - £12} = 700 \text{ units}$$

This shows that 700 units must be made and sold to bring the firm to the break-even point. The difference between unit price and unit direct or variable cost is £10. This £10 is what is termed the unit contribution. The first 700 units contribute £7,000 towards the recovery of the fixed costs of the firm. As the £12 direct costs have been recovered in arriving at the £10 contribution, this means that at 700 units the firm has a break-even point. If the firm makes and sells the 1,000 units shown in the budget for the year, then the remaining 300 units will provide £3,000 contribution to profit.

Such calculations provide an easy check that the correct break-even point has been found:

Break-even volume	700 units equals	zero profit
Balance left of budget	300 units at £10 per unit =	£3,000 profit
Budget sales	1,000 units with profit of	£3,000

If it is necessary to calculate the break-even point not in terms of units to be made and sold, but in the amount of sales revenue, then there are two methods which can be adopted. The first is to relate the sales price to the contribution and use this as a multiple on the fixed costs:

$$
\begin{array}{ll}
\text{Price} & \text{£}22 \\
\text{Variable costs} & \underline{12} \\
\text{Contribution} & \underline{10} \\
& \underline{\text{£}22}
\end{array}
$$

$$
\frac{\text{Price £}22}{\text{Contribution £}10} = 2.2
$$

Fixed costs (£7,000) x 2.2 = £15,400
(700 units at a price of £22 = £15,400)

This provides a sales revenue of £15,400 for the break-even level.

The second method is to calculate the contribution percentage and use this rather than the unit contribution in the break-even formula. The contribution percentage in .this case is:

$$
\frac{\text{Contribution £}10}{\text{Price £}22} \text{ x } 100 = 45.45\%
$$

Applying this in the break-even formula:

$$
\frac{\text{Fixed costs £}7,000}{\text{Contribution percentage .}4545} = \text{£}15,400
$$

Having used one of these methods to discover the break-even point of operations, it is worth comparing the break-even volume with the sales budget. In this case, it can be seen that 70% of the sales budget must be achieved before the company begins to make a profit. This gives some indication of the 'margin of safety' of the product. If it is considered that the break-even volume is too high a percentage of the sales budget – i.e. there is too small a margin of safety — then management may consider whether it is possible to reduce the fixed costs or to change the direct costs or price in order to provide a better situation.

Having completed the description of break-even analysis and introduced the concept of contribution, it is now possible to move towards an assessment of marginal costing. In most situations it is possible to say that:

Marginal costing = Direct costing = Variable costing
$$= \text{Contribution analysis}$$

Where companies separate their variable costs of output and sale from the fixed expenses, then they are adopting some form of marginal costing. The accountant is forced to make the assumption that the marginal cost of a product is the same as the variable costs that can be set against that product. However, in real life there will always be differences in the manner in which companies treat various types of cost. For example, though in the current example labour has been treated as a completely variable cost, this is often not the case, as a team of skilled employees may in effect be a fixed cost for their company. They cannot be fired and hired as need indicates, but must be maintained intact throughout long periods.

Marginal costing is often associated in the manager's mind with declining prices, cut-throat competition and low profits, but it is a very useful concept and can provide quick pointers in decision-making situations. One area where it is extensively used is in export marketing. The result of its application was described by one marketing manager thus: 'When we use it on them, it's good business; when they use it on us, it's dumping.'

To illustrate its application in such situations, consider the situation where the firm that has been used as an example so far has sold 800 units of the product for £22, and in the last few weeks of the year sees the potential market dry up for that product and is unable to sell any more. They are then offered the chance to sell 100 units at £18. Had the firm been using full costing, then it can be seen from p. 148 that the cost would have been shown as £19 per unit, and so the order would probably have been rejected. But what would the real impact on profitability be?

The unit contribution has now become £6 (price £18 less direct costs £12), and as the company has already passed the break-even point in sales, this £6 is a contribution to profit. Thus, selling 100 units at £18 will provide an additional £600 profit:

Profit on 800 units	£1,000	(£10 x 100 units)
Profit on 100 units	600	(£6 x 100 units)
Total profit	£1,600	

Indeed, as long as the product is sold at something above its marginal cost of £12, then this will contribute to profit once the break-even volume has been reached.

It is in this manner that marginal costing can be applied to export marketing. If the firm considered it possible to sell 1,000 units on the home market with a price of £22 to provide the required profit level of £3,000, and there were still some spare capacity available for further production of the product without incurring any additional fixed costs, then it might consider selling in another market overseas. As long as a price of over £12 were achieved (assuming no additional costs of transporting the product to the new markets), then overall profit would be increased. It would be possible for the same product to be offered in two separate markets at vastly different prices and yet each market be profitable for the firm concerned. Where there is capacity available, then marginal cost pricing is a useful method of providing extra income for a firm.

There are, of course, problems with the application of marginal costing in the pricing decision. If a firm were to sell its product at a marginal cost price at the end of the financial year just to increase profits for that year, it might find resistance when it tried to bring its price back to normal at the beginning of the following year. Also, it is most important that managers understand that even though a product may be returning a contribution, that in no way guarantees that the total contribution will be sufficient to cover the fixed costs associated with that product, let alone provide a profit. Just because there is a contribution does not mean there will automatically be a profit. For example, if all 1,000 units of the product used in the examples so far had been sold at a price of £18, which provides a unit contribution of £6, the situation at the year-end would have been:

Revenue 1,000 units at £18		= £18,000	
Direct costs	£12,000		*loss* £1,000
Indirect costs	£7,000	£19,000	

At a price of £18 the break-even point is 1,167 units or £21,000 revenue. The fact that a unit contribution does not ensure an overall profit is not the only problem with marginal cost pricing. There have been several cases where a firm has exported its product at a very low price using the approach shown previously, and then found that a keen-eyed business-man has brought these same products back to the home market to sell them at a lower price than the company charges. As the products are identical in all respects, this can be embarrassing for the company concerned. Thus, the use of marginal cost for pricing and profit decisions must be very carefully controlled if these practical problems are to be avoided. It is never marginal costing that creates the problems, but the application.

One way in which contribution analysis can be of assistance in a pricing situation is where it is being considered whether or not to reduce the price of a product. It is quite often argued that if the price is brought down, this will result in an increased sales volume and greater profitability. The first calculation that should be done under these circum-stances is to discover how much increased volume is required to stand still, i.e. to make the same profit as is planned under the existing price. This can be done as follows:

It is suggested that if the price of the product is reduced from £22 to £17 there will be increased sales and profitability for the firm.

$$\text{Units} = \frac{\text{Fixed costs £7,000 + Planned profit £3,000}}{\text{Unit price £17 } - \text{ Unit variable cost £12}}$$

$$= \frac{£10,000}{£5}$$

$$= 2,000$$

Conclusion: To make the same profit as was planned with a price of £22 it will be necessary to produce and sell twice the quantity of the product.

The break-even formula has been used not to find the number of units that will produce zero profit, but the number to be made and sold to make the profit that was originally planned of £3,000. With this information, management can consider whether it is worth the effort of doubling production and sales for the same profit level as previously. However, if they consider it possible to sell 3,000 units, then the resulting profit of £8,000 may well be attractive. But there may also be considerations of capacity involved — perhaps the fixed costs will be increased to enable greater production volumes to be attained. In this case, clearly the volume needed to produce £3,000 profit will be even greater.

The adoption of marginal costing and contribution analysis acts to focus attention on those factors that are important and relevant to a decision. To illustrate this, consider the following financial statement on the three products made and sold by a firm:

	A £'000	B £'000	C £'000	Total £'000
Sales revenue	900	600	300	1,800
Cost of goods sold:				
Variable	390	295	205	890
Fixed	150	100	50	300
Selling expenses:				
Variable	80	60	70	210
Fixed	75	50	25	150
Total costs	695	505	350	1,550
Pre-tax profit/loss	205	95	(50)	250

From this report it would appear that the product C is unprofitable and management could decide to drop its distribution, thus increasing overall profit by £50,000. But is this really the case? Has management got the right information upon which to base their decision? To both these questions the answer is no. One way of presenting the financial information in a better form for a true understanding of product C's viability is as follows:

	A £'000	B £'000	C £'000	Total £'000
Sales revenue	900	600	300	1,800
Variable costs:				
Cost of goods sold	390	295	205	890
Selling expenses	80	60	70	210
Contribution	430	245	25	700
Fixed costs				450
Pre-tax profit				£250

Setting the information out in this format highlights the total contribution to fixed costs and eventual profit that each product generates and provides the basis for a more detailed analysis and a more satisfactory decision on product C.

It can be seen that product C provides £25,000 contribution to fixed costs and profit. Thus, if this product is dropped and there follows no reduction in the total fixed costs, then the firm will make £25,000 less profit than at present. This is because the fixed costs will have to be absorbed by the two remaining products A and B. The £50,000 loss shown for C will go, but the £75,000 fixed costs it is bearing will remain.

The decision can now focus on the basic question of how much fixed costs really relate to product C. In the original financial analysis, fixed costs have been allocated on the basis of sales revenue (9:6:3), but it is most unlikely that this truly represents the incurring of such costs. Allocating fixed costs on the basis of revenue in effect assumes that an increase in revenue (which could be brought about by a price increase) will automatically increase the fixed costs associated with that product. If different methods of allocation were used, a different spread of profit would be shown between the three products. Indeed, it would be possible to make the profit appear under any one of the products, depending on the arbitrary allocation method chosen. Using the contribution approach removes this difficulty, as the fixed costs are not allocated to individual products but merely shown as a deduction from the overall contribution.

If management discover that more than £25,000 of fixed costs will be eliminated if product C is dropped, then the firm will make more profit than if it maintained distribution of this product. If less than £25,000 fixed costs will be lost, then the firm is better off keeping product C.

This type of analysis can also be applied to the assessment of divisional performance. It is not unusual to find reporting systems in companies which compare the profitability and general performance of divisions with the head office expenses allocated on some arbitrary basis between the divisions. This obscures the real situation. Had the three products in the previous example been three divisions in a company and the fixed expenses been those of head office, then the problem would have been the same. Division C appears to be less profitable than the other divisions. For a clear picture of the situation it is essential that arbitrary allocations of fixed costs be avoided. Management in divisions should only be judged on the costs and revenues that they can control. If division C were making no use of head office services, then it is better to judge it on the basis of a £25,000 contribution than a £50,000 loss.

A further discussion of control, analysis and assessment of performance is provided in Chapter 9 dealing with budgetary control.

8.5. Contribution and Pricing
In the previous section of this chapter the use of marginal cost in pricing was mentioned, but there is no reason to limit its use to the export situation.

The argument is often put forward by managers that in order to set a price it is necessary to know the full cost of the product being dealt with. This is particularly strongly advocated where there is divisional responsibility for price-setting. In a case like the example in section 8.4 where the three divisions A, B and C were used, managers tend to prefer to have head office expenses allocated to divisions so that the divisional manager knows what costs he must recover to make a 'profit'. It is difficult to accept this point of view. It means that managers are incapable of getting the best price for their products without a full costing basis. Certainly all costs must be recovered before a profit is made, but fixed costs should only have a limited impact on the pricing decision. The logical conclusion would be the situation in which a head office with several divisions of a company would allocate a much greater amount of 'fixed costs' to each division so as to ensure even higher profitability. The allocation of fixed costs only tends to provide a psychological crutch to management in the pricing decision. If they aim to maximise overall contribution from their products, they will automatically get the best profit available.

9 Budgetary Control and Corporate Planning

In the previous two chapters cost behaviour and costing systems were discussed. In this chapter budgeting and budgetary control are considered. The word 'budget' comes from the French for a small bag or purse, and came to be associated with the Chancellor of the Exchequer's bag, which contains his annual estimate of the country's income and expenditure in the national budget. The Chancellor is concerned with planning, co-ordinating and controlling income and expenditure for the government. For a manager in a business firm there are the same tasks to be faced. Budgeting has for many years been seen as aid in this process.

A simple diagrammatic representation of the manager's job will illustrate where, and how, the budgeting system can assist:

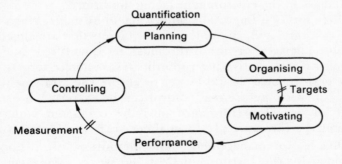

One of the main functions of a manager is to plan — to decide what is to be done, and how it is to be carried out or achieved. If the manager is a senior executive in the firm, then he will have the task of considering the overall objectives of the firm, and setting the plan for their achievement for the firm as a whole. If the manager has responsibility for a function in the firm, then he will probably be given guidance as to what he should try to achieve, but be left freedom as to how it is achieved. The question of corporate objectives is discussed in more detail in the first section of this chapter.

Once he has decided what is to be achieved within the time period under consideration, and has formulated a plan, the manager must organise the human and physical resources at his disposal in order that the plan may be carried out. The human resources will require some motivation to strive for the attainment of the manager's plans, whereas the plant and machinery will just require plugging in to the power source. Behavioural aspects of budgeting and control are considered later in this chapter.

With the human and physical resources co-ordinated, responsibility for actual performance of the various tasks is allotted. Products are produced and distributed, or services provided, depending upon the nature of the firm's business. As time proceeds, the manager monitors performance and assesses how far it has gone towards the achievement of the plan, and takes any necessary control action. Often it will be necessary to adjust plans in the light of changed experience or changes in the environment facing the firm.

There are two important points yet to be made. When the plan is formulated, the objectives or targets that are aimed at by the manager or the firm must be quantified, and in organising and motivating subordinates, concrete targets for their performance should be set to ensure the attainment of the plan. Also, before real control can be exercised measurement of actual performance must be compared with the planned performance. It is in these areas that budgets are invaluable to management. The definition of a budget provided by the Institute of Cost and Works (Management) Accountants in an introductory text is: 'A financial and/or quantitative statement, prepared prior to a defined period of time, of policy to be pursued during that period for the purpose of attaining a given objective.' A budget is a systematic statement of the firm's intentions over a specified period of time, normally one year, which should enable the firm's objectives to be achieved. Though it is most common that budgets be expressed in financial terms, there is no necessity for this. The budget should be set in terms that are meaningful to the organisation and the individual manager concerned.

The first step in any budgeting activity is to decide what it is that the firm is trying to achieve through its operations, and it is to the definition of corporate objectives that attention is first directed.

9.1. Corporate Objectives and Budgeting

Budgeting is concerned with planning, co-ordinating and controlling, but in order to carry out these activities there must be an objective that is the basis for all the work undertaken. The plan, whether it is strategic or tactical, is concerned with the 'how', not with the 'what'. A plan or budget can only be formulated once the objective is clearly defined.

As far as the business firm is concerned, it is often stated that all that matters is profit, and that this is therefore the objective of the firm — indeed, the reason for its existence. For many years theoretical economists insisted that profit maximisation was the main objective of a business. But unfortunately it is not as simple as this. There are many other factors that must be taken into account in planning in business. Not the least of the problems with profit is the time scale against which it is to be set. Over what period is the firm 'maximising' profit? It may be possible to make a large profit today, but at the sacrifice of long-term profitability, or even survival.

In the late 1950s and early 1960s several major American companies tackled the problem of corporate objectives. One such company which has provided a tremendous amount of information on both its success and failure in this area is General Electric. Together with several leading management consultants and academics, this company developed a series of 'key areas' that any firm must consider in looking to the future. These key areas are:

— market standing
— innovation
— productivity

— profitability
— management development
— employee attitudes
— public responsibility
— balance between short- and long-term activities

The list places the key areas in no particular ranked order. All areas are equally important and all require consideration by management; none can be ignored. If any firm falls down in one of the key areas, then it puts its entire operations in jeopardy. Of course, the description of the key areas provided in the minimum words possible in the list above must be adapted to the particular firm concerned, but this in no way affects their importance.

Market standing is related to the question of sales volume. Every firm offering a product for sale is concerned with the penetration made by that product into the overall market. Where possible, this can be measured by reference to the market share obtained, but otherwise an assessment of volume is necessary. The firm's intentions in this respect must be clarified, as they have a direct relationship with the forecasting of sales revenue.

The firm may also be interested in achieving or maintaining some form of product leadership. This may be done through technical innovation which is the result of research and development carried out by the firm. In the case of General Electric there was a clear intention to be first in the field with new products or innovations on existing product lines. A firm that has no such aims must still clarify its intentions in this area. Is it merely going to match competition, or concentrate on some other form of product leadership, such as offering the best value for money to customers?

Productivity is of vital importance to any organisation. The better the relationship between input and output, the more efficiently the firm is operating. A firm must assess how its productivity may best be measured, or which are the key functions where productivity is important.

Profitability is a key factor in any business, and one which is always given close attention by management. The profit area is directly related to the previous three key areas. There is a direct interrelationship between them all. Market share, which may be obtained through innovation, produces revenue, and productivity ensures efficient use of resources and eventual profit levels.

Management development is critical in any organisation. There is little point in planning for growth if there is not going to be sufficient managers to run the firm when it increases in size. The human resources of a firm are in many ways the most important. It is the managers that enable the firm to be run effectively and to achieve its objectives.

The other employees in the firm are also important. The way in which they view their work and management can have a direct impact on productivity and profitability. Their attitudes must be known by management if they are to be deployed effectively and profitably.

General Electric was one of the first firms to recognise the importance of public responsibility as a corporate objective. The company must recognise that it is a citizen of the community in which it operates. It has a duty not only to provide continued employment but also to maintain the 'rules' of the community. Today, with the great emphasis on avoiding pollution, this has even more relevance. The firm can no longer afford to ignore its environment, but must legally as well as morally accept its place and obligations in society.

The final key area in the list is also very important. Every firm, and every manager, must always be watchful that actions or policy are not set in motion that produce immediate favourable results but have an adverse impact in the longer term. For example, a firm may decide that it can improve profitability by reducing the quality of its products. In the short term this may well be the case, but the longer-term implications of this decision may be to alienate its customers, bringing about lower profitability. Every decision and policy statement must be considered not only in the light of its current impact but also as to its longer-term effects on the business as a whole.

All these key areas have a connection with the financial resources of the company. Executive management will have to consider how their plans are to be financed and what the plans' implications are for cash flow during the period of their operation. Often finance will in the end be the main constraint or limiting factor for all the others. As a result, finance will be a separate key area for management consideration.

For effective planning and eventual budgeting, management must consider each of these key areas. Often this will result in a decision that an area has no applicability to the firm and therefore can be discounted. However, the exercise of assessing a key area's importance is valuable in itself for management. There is danger chiefly where management ignores a key area by default, not when this is done after careful assessment.

Where the key areas are relevant to a firm, then objectives must be framed to set out in clear terms management's intentions in each area. The objectives must have certain attributes if they are to be worthwhile and capable of being incorporated into a sound budgeting system. The basic requirements for a valid objective are that it:

- act as a guide to specific action by those concerned
- be capable of measurement
- be ambitious enough to challenge
- take account of all internal and external constraints
- be related to the higher and lower objectives in that area.

Management must discuss such questions as 'What business are we really in?', 'Where do we want to be as a firm in five years' time?', and 'How do we get there?' The answers must be set in the light of the external and internal constraints that will restrict success, and what the strengths and weaknesses of the firm are which can be exploited or overcome.

Conflict is inevitable in this situation, but unless the conflict is resolved, a firm may find itself striving for conflicting objectives, and almost certainly see different sections of the firm pulling in opposite directions. The sales manager may look for large discounts, many products and immediate delivery to any point in the country. Conversely, the production manager may want few products, larger volumes and longer runs. Other line and staff managers may be looking for other factors which compound the problem. Unless such conflict is resolved or contained, it can become destructive to the firm. The objectives of the firm must be clearly stated and distributed to all managers in order that they may see what it is they are trying to achieve. This can provide the basis for comprehensive and effective budgetary control procedures.

9.2. Budgetary Control

Simply stated, budgetary control is a system where budgets are prepared for the various activities of a firm, and actual performance is continually compared with that budget. To be fully effective, the budgetary control system must be devised with close attention to the organisational structure of the firm. The budgets should be set for the various separate responsibility centres of the firm. A budget for a manager should consist of a formal statement of the various resources at his disposal, how they are to be used during the period covered by the budget, and what is expected to be the end result of their deployment. Budgets are normally expressed in financial terms and all the individual responsibility centres brought together in a Master Budget which is a Profit and Loss Statement and Balance Sheet for the end of the budget period. However, individual managers may have their own sections of the overall budget put into terms which are relevant to their responsibilities, and it is left to the accountant to translate these into financial terms when necessary.

Having started the budgeting procedure by defining the overall objectives of the firm, the next stage is to prepare a series of statements which set out the key responsibility areas' intended actions for the budgeting period. These individual budgets are interrelated and in total offer a budget Profit and Loss Account and Balance Sheet, as illustrated in Fig. 9.1.

There is often a problem as to where to start the budgeting process. Commonly the easiest starting-point is with sales. Sales tend to be the limiting factor for the majority of firms

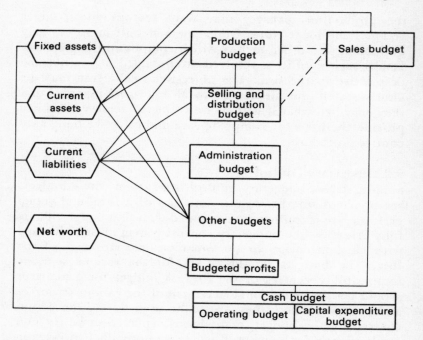

in that there is a constraint as to how much can be sold of the product or how much service can be offered. There is no reason why this should apply in every case, but a firm should start with the key factor that can act to limit operations. In some circumstances this may be productive capacity where a firm is limited not by what it can sell, but by what it can produce, and in this situation it is the starting-point for the budgeting process.

Where sales are the limiting factor, then the managers responsible for selling the products or services are faced with the task of preparing a sales forecast for the coming period: what are they going to sell, when it it to be sold, where is it to be sold, and who is going to sell it. It is easier if initially only the physical side of sales is considered, as these figures must be agreed with the productive resources of the firm. There is little point in budgeting to sell what it is physically impossible for the production unit to supply. Once the physical requirements of sales have been agreed with the productive capabilities, then these can be put into financial terms. The price at which products are to be sold is multiplied by the volume of sales to arrive at revenue for the period, and the cost of selling and distribution calculated.

In order to prepare a sales forecast, the manager must have some idea of the potential market for the products he is selling. This will involve a knowledge of who the firm's customers are, what competition there is or will be, and how price will affect demand. One useful concept from economic theory that can be applied in this area is that of price elasticity — how volume will change as the price is increased or reduced. Two typical price/demand curves are shown below. That on the left illustrates a typical situation where demand increases as the price is reduced. A less common situation is shown on the right where if too low a price is set, there is suspicion that the product is of poor quality and so demand is low; as the price is raised, confidence is created and more are sold until too high a price is reached and volume decreases again. Shopkeepers are well aware of this second curve, which illustrated that price can be an indicator of quality to customers. If there are two boxes of identical apples set side by side, one box at 10p per lb and one at 20p per lb, sometimes most customers will buy the higher-priced apples 'because they are better quality'. Knowing the

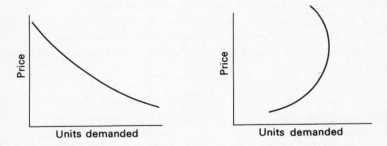

sensitivity of demand and volume to price is essential in sales forecasting. If the knowledge is used in conjunction with the concepts of break-even analysis and contribution set out in Chapter 8, then sales revenue and profit can be more finely judged and budgeted.

The sales forcast and budget will be dependent upon many factors over which the firm has no real control. There will be political and economic factors impinging on the sales capability of the firm, and whilst the firm cannot control these factors, they must be taken into account in drafting the sales budget. It is firmly recommended that all assumptions relating to forecasts be formally stated in the budget in order that they may be discussed and agreed by all concerned rather than left unknown or disputed. One of the big dangers to effective budgeting is where assumptions about future events are not clearly communicated to all concerned. An assumption made in preparing the sales forecast will have a bearing on the work done in preparing the production budget and the selling and distribution budgets that are to be felt at all levels and in all functions of the firm.

The production budget will be based upon the requirements for fulfilling the sales budget, and will commence with an assessment as to the physical capabilities of the production to meet these needs. There will be consideration not only of production capacity but also of changes to be made in the inventory levels of finished goods. Purchasing needs will be placed in the budget, as will labour requirements. Capital investment programmes necessary to allow production to attain the required level must also be budgeted. Then all these figures are quantified into a production cost budget which can be set against the sales revenue budget.

The following list summarises the information required for, and contained in, the sales and production budgets. These two form the lock into which other sub-budgets are keyed.

Sales Budget	*Production Budget*
Initial requirements	*Initial requirements*
Products to be sold	Productive capacity
Sales force available	Inventory — materials
Competitive activities	— work-in-progress
Areas where products sold	— finished goods
Type of customers	Labour force available
Environmental factors	Physical sales requirements
	— timing
	— type of product

Producing the budget	*Producing the budget*
Sales forecast	Sales forecast budget
— timing	— timing
— quantity	— nature of product
— customer	— quantity
— area	Materials purchasing budget
Marketing plan	Direct labour budget
Advertising and promotion plan	Overhead budget
Selling and distribution plan	Capital investment budget

Sales Budget   Inventory Budget   Production Budget

These budgets are quantified in financial terms by the accountant to bring into the assessment such factors as cash flow, credit policy, discount structure and price, together with delivery lead times, stock level calculations and credit taken from suppliers. At this stage gross profit levels can be seen, and any necessary adjustments made before finalisation of the budgets. However, it is not only profit that management is considering in this exercise, but also the cash flow. As set out in Chapter 3, cash budgeting is just as critical as profit planning in a firm, and the cash budget is given prime importance as a reflection in cash terms of the various budgets. There is little point in a firm finalising a set of budgets if financial constraints make them impossible. This is the major contribution that the accountant can offer in the budgeting process. Managers present their own budgets in terms meaningful to them; the accountant translates them into financial terms, and brings them all together in a profit statement and a cash budget.

The other areas in which budgets are prepared, such as administration, research and development, and general expense, follow a similar pattern of development. For example, the personnel and training manager will develop a budget which reflects the requirements of both the sales and production budgets. Employees will be recruited and trained to fulfil the firm's needs, and there will be a general ongoing set of expenses to maintain the personnel function in operation. All these will be budgeted and set into financial terms by the accountant for eventual incorporation into both the profit statement and the cash budget.

9.3. Administration of a Budgetary Control System

So far it is the mechanical side of budgeting that has been considered, but a significant part of budgetary control is concerned with the initiation of budgets, their agreement by senior executives, and their implementation by the managers concerned.

It is essential if effective budgetary control is to be achieved that the managers are involved, that they participate in the setting of the budgets that relate to their responsibilities and activities. The manager — often the accountant — who starts the budgeting procedure may call upon the various functional managers to draft their budget proposals for the coming period. The manner in which this is compiled will vary from firm to firm but, as an example, with a sales manager the steps might be as follows:

- (i) Collect all available historic information on previous sales
    - — by product
    - — by area
    - — by customer
    - — by time.
- (ii) Ensure full appreciation of overall objectives of the firm in so far as they affect sales levels.
- (iii) Ask area/product sales manager for their assessment of the coming period's sales potential in the same classifications as given in (i) above.
- (iv) Bring this information together and assess its implications for profit and for production requirements.
- (v) Meet with all senior sales managers to discuss (iv).
- (vi) Agree and set sales budgets for the various managers' responsibility areas.

Throughout this process the accountant will be involved in presenting the possible sales strategies and policies in financial-terms both for cash flow and profitability. If any new products are to be introduced, their launch will be programmed into the sales budget as well as the cash flow forecast.

Once the sales manager is satisfied with his budget he will

present it to executive management, or the other managers in the firm, for discussion and eventual agreement. The sales budget will be set in the context of the other budgets and related to overall profitability and cash availability. For each budget area the manager concerned should present both his assumptions and planned actions for approval, and once approval has been received the budget then becomes the main guide to the manager's activities for the coming period. The budget is what the manager is trying to achieve, and he has responsibility for its success. If there is failure then the manager can be called to account, and asked to provide reasons for not meeting the budget.

As with standard costing, which was outlined in Chapter 7, a decision must be taken as to what level of attainment is expected in the budgets. Is it to be based on previous years' experience, probably providing an easy level of attainment for the manager; is an ideal level to be set that can only be achieved with perfect conditions and maximum efficiency; or is a level set that is possible, but which will require considerable effort to attain? The problems of budgets and motivation are considered later in this chapter.

9.4. Reporting under Budgetary Control

If a system of budgeting is to be of any real value in a firm, there must be complete commitment to it from the senior executives concerned. The budgeting system of itself will not guarantee any better results or better control, unless it is used properly. While much benefit can be obtained just from the exercise of producing budgets, real benefits can be obtained by their effective implementation. Managers must see that budgets are taken seriously, and when they fall short of their own particular section of the budget they themselves should be called to account.

At regular intervals, at least monthly, managers should receive a statement setting their actual performance against budget, and analysing variances to show whether they are favourable or adverse, and how they arose. Was it due to price changes or volume changes as described under standard costing variance analysis in Chapter 7?

A great deal of benefit can be derived from showing the

Units

Product	This month				Year to date				To year-end		
	Budget	Actual	+/-	%	Budget	Actual	+/-	%	Budget	Actual	Remaining
A	100	110	10	10	800	900	100	13	1,000	900	100
B	100	90	(10)	(10)	900	1,000	100	11	1,000	1,000	—
C	100	80	(20)	(20)	700	600	(100)	(14)	900	600	300
. . .											

Revenue (£)

Product	This month				Year to date				To year-end		
	Budget	Actual	+/-	%	Budget	Actual	+/-	%	Budget	Actual	Remaining
A	1,000	1,060	60	6	8,000	9,100	1,100	14	12,000	9,100	2,900
B	1,000	840	(160)	(16)	7,000	8,200	800	11	10,000	8,200	1,800
C	1,000	700	(300)	(30)	9,000	8,700	(300)	(3)	12,000	8,700	3,300
. . .											

variances from budget not only in financial or other quantified terms, but also as percentages, as shown opposite. A sales manager armed with this sort of budget and actual information has a useful tool. There is set out the current month's activity, figures for the year to date, and also what must still be achieved if the year-end results are to match those budgeted.

In reporting under budgetary control systems it is important to split the reports into two sections: the first dealing with factors over which the manager concerned has some direct control (as in the example above), and the second dealing with the various non-controllable factors such as rates, insurance, depreciation, etc. There is little to be gained from demanding detailed explanations for variances of factors over which the manager has no direct control. The only time it is useful to compare budget with actual for the non-controllable factors is when it is the overall administration and general overhead budget that is being considered and the report is being sent to the manager(s) responsible for this area in the firm.

One decision the firm must make with variance analysis — whether it be standard costing or budgeting variances — is what level of variance is significant and worthy of investigation. Budgetary control allows management by exception — that is, management's attention is drawn to the fact that things have not turned out as was planned. But if every variance of any size is investigated, the system will grind to a halt or fall into complete disregard by functional managers. Management may set a level of ±10% as being the minimum level of variance that they will investigate, but obviously it will depend on which section of operations is under assessment. It is possible to use simple statistical techniques to provide control limits for variances. By this means it would be possible to calculate to a given confidence level (99.8% or 95%, for example) within which results would be expected to fall. Where actual results fall beyond this band, then investigation is undertaken. This sort of analysis is particularly effective for repetitive production activities, but of less value for monitoring sales activity.

The graphical presentation of budget and actual performance data can provide a quick and easy means of identifying problem areas for further investigation. For example, the graph illustrated below shows current year's sales revenue expressed as a percentage change from the budgeted sales for the year. This allows a much quicker appreciation of deviations from budget than studying a series of tables, and could be maintained as a wall chart in the manager's office and updated regularly.

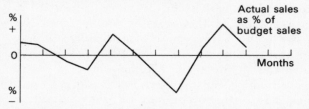

The second graph shows selling and distribution expenses as a percentage of sales revenue, and allows speedy isolation of changes which require explanation.

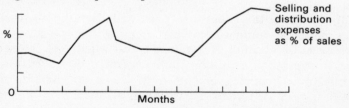

This same graphical approach can be used to monitor current assets by comparing actual levels with those budgeted, as set out below:

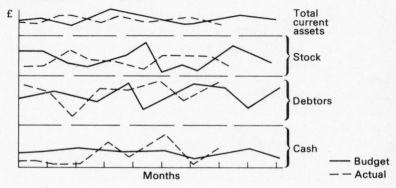

With this graph the budgeted levels for cash, debtors and stock are compared with actual levels experienced. This does not present any different information than is contained in a typical budget report, but it does set it out in a manner that can be quickly appreciated and followed by any manager.

One final illustration of the use of graphs in management control and reporting is with moving annual totals and cumulative differences. A moving annual total (MAT) is found by taking the previous eleven months' results and adding the current month's, then dividing by twelve. This is done each month, and if the changes between the MATs are studied this can show a trend developing in the area to which it is applied. If this is put into graphical form, the results are simple to follow. A cumulative difference graph is illustrated below:

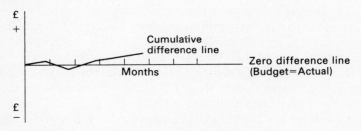

This graph shows the cumulative differences between actual performance and budgeted performance. If actual is exactly the same as budget, then there will be no difference, but as each month shows a difference this is added to the difference for the year to date, and plotted on the graph. This again allows quick awareness of changes or trends developing in the area graphed which call for further management attention and action. Once the cumulative difference line is seen to continue to move away from the zero difference line, then this can indicate a trend that should be investigated. It is also possible to introduce control limit lines into this graph to indicate with greater precision the development of a trend.

No manager should feel constrained by the traditional reporting system in operation in a firm. It is the manager's duty to ensure that information is presented in a manner which is capable of appreciation in the minimum time, and in the best form for the method of control to be exercised. In many firms it has been proved that graphical presentation is both quick and simple to prepare — it requires no more information than the ordinary accounting/budgeting reports, nor does it require great skill in drafting — and with graphs managers visually understand better what is happening in their area of responsibility than under any other method of presentation.

9.5. Some Problems with Budgetary Control

In recent years there has been considerable interest in the behavioural implications of budgetary control systems — the manner in which individuals react to having budgets set, and their performance against those budgets measured. The way in which managers accept a budgeting system can affect the manner in which they approach their work. It is not unusual to find that middle managers see a budgetary control system as almost entirely for monitoring their personal performance rather than as a tool to allow more effective management. A firm must be careful to ensure that managers really appreciate the need for a formal control system if they are to function efficiently, and that it is not solely to measure their personal achievements. Where a budgeting system is tied to a bonus system the problems are compounded by introducing a separate motivation to managers to beat the budget. Once managers see budgeting as a static formal efficiency measure, then budgetary control becomes like a complicated game with unwritten rules. Managers will 'weight' their budgets in order to ensure sufficient leeway to guarantee that they can at least meet their budget. Enterprise, originality and flair are channelled into defeating the system, to the detriment of the success of the firm.

One particular problem that is frequently encountered in budgeting is where budgets are based on an estimated volume of output and then that volume is not achieved, so that the budget is exceeded or not met. How are the actual results compared in any meaningful manner with the budget when the basis for comparison is missing? There is an answer to this where flexible budgeting is used. Under a system of flexible budgeting, costs and revenues are analysed to see how they react to volume changes, and then when the volume changes they are 'flexed' or recalculated to meet this volume change. The actual performance figures are then compared with the budget figures that relate to the volumes achieved during the period, and meaningful variances produced. An example of this is provided below:

	Budget volume 1,000 hours	Other volumes 1,100	1,200	1,300	
Indirect labour	700	700	750	800	800
Maintenance	100	100	120	130	150
Power	100	110	120	130	110
Depreciation, etc	100	100	100	100	100
	£1,000	£1,010	£1,090	£1,160	£1,160

If the actual costs of £1,160 are compared with a static budget level of £1,000 and 1,000 hours (£1 per hour worked), then there will be a favourable variance of £40 disclosed:

1,200 hours worked at £1 per hour	£1,200
Actual cost incurred	£1,160
	£40

However, if the actual cost is compared with what should have been incurred at 1,200 hours of work, then an adverse variance of £70 is shown:

Flexible budget figure for 1,200 hours	£1,090
Actual costs at 1,200 hours worked	£1,600
	−£70

In this manner better information can be prepared for management decisions and action. Budgeting must be dynamic if it is to provide real benefit to a firm and allow managers useful control information. The production of useless variances is the factor most likely to turn managers against budgeting. Budgets must relate to their operational activities when comparison is made with actual performance.

In 1971 E. H. Caplan published a book *Management Accounting and Behavioural Science* (Reading, Mass., 1971) which was based on considerable research in this area. It was shown that there were deep conflicts between the assumptions accountants were making in the traditional accounting control system in a firm and the theory and observations of behavioural scientists. These assumptions can be listed as:

— assumptions concerning organisational objectives
— assumptions as to human behaviour
— assumptions in the management accounting system.

In a traditional system accountants assume that the chief business objective is to maximise profit. This is clearly not the real case as firms are complex organisations with many objectives which may be in conflict. Firms are also made up of groups of individuals each having their own personal ambitions and objectives, as well as ways of looking at their firm. The way in which these people react is vital to the firm's directions and the balance of the controlling group may change, bringing about changes in the overall objectives of the firm. These facts must be accepted in a realistic budgeting system. A firm has many objectives, often conflicting, that change over time.

It is often assumed that people are only motivated by money, and would prefer not to have to work for a living. Thus, a manager is felt to be faced with lazy employees who must be controlled, and motivated, by money. This is by no means true. as motivation differs from individual to individual and the importance attached to money rewards is by no means constant.

It is thought that the management accounting system is mainly trying to assist management to maximise profits, identify bad performance, and allocate targets with accurate information and a neutral approach. This is debatable even if one ignores the profit maximisation argument. The main purpose of a system is to provide a communication network in a firm, and to allow adequate information to all levels of management so as to facilitate planning and control. The system itself is not necessarily neutral, as accountants have a wide discretion in how they present their information, and can also be influenced by their own personal or departmental objectives.

Budgetary control is a simple technique to understand, but its operation is very complex for it brings many factors together. The manager operating budgetary control must be aware of the behavioural implications of the system and constantly bear in mind that it is people he is dealing with. Every manager has a distinct managerial style, and in every firm the manner in which budgets are used is different, not from the formal process but from the way in which the budgets are set, operated and used. The manager must choose the method of implementation in budgetary control which best suits the firm and the management style of those concerned. People must not be lost in the figures, or a poor result is bound to ensue.

9.6. PPBS and Zero-Base Budgeting
The U.S. Department of Defence introduced a system of budgeting that was intended to improve the existing system by concentrating on the output of the department, improving the pre-allocation budgeting together with quicker estimates of requirements, and looking further ahead than just one or two years. This was called program planning and budgeting systems (PPBS), and has rapidly been taken over for use in government agencies all over the world in the last decade. PPBS requires that the objectives of the organisation be clearly defined, and that all feasible alternative means of achieving these objectives be considered. A cost—benefit analysis is then done to choose the most effective alternative. The system is particularly useful in government agencies, but can equally well be used in larger organisations.

In the late 1960s and early 1970s Texas Instruments in America developed a system of budgeting termed 'zero-base budgeting'. This was developed from a need to reduce overall budgets in a particular year, and management was asked what they would cut in order to meet the reduced budget level in that year. It was then considered worthwhile to discover exactly what the various units in the firm were going to do during the year. From this there arose a system by which each year management is required to produce a minimum level of activity budget for their operations that would cover the absolute minimum requirements to maintain an acceptable operating level, and then on top of this to prepare a series of 'decision packages' for levels above this. These decision packages show how additional funds would be used if they were available, and what the end return would be from each package. The packages are ranked in order of importance for the department or division, thus enabling management to assess what will be produced if extra funds are allotted, and to make an objective allocation to departments of available resources beyond the minimum requirements. This system forces managers to re-evaluate all expenditures each year, and to justify their budget on the basis of what will be returned to the firm if they receive it.

Appendix 1: European Accounting Practices

It is sometimes erroneously assumed that European accounting does not match that of the United States for accuracy or informative presentation. There are differences between European and American presentation practice, and in the amount of information required under statute, but the underlying principles that were set out at the beginning of this book are accepted and used in all countries which have a recognised body of professional accountants. Accountants share the same body of common knowledge and tend to approach financial reporting in a similar manner.

The purpose of this appendix is to provide a manager with sufficient background information about the differing approaches to financial accounting in the major European countries to enable an appreciation of the published information available on companies in these countries to be made. Any language problems will, needless to say, have to be solved to the best of the manager's ability when he is faced with a set of real-life foreign accounts. The countries are dealt with in alphabetical order.

1. Belgium

There are two recognised bodies of auditors in Belgium, the Reviseurs d'Entreprises and the Reviseurs de Banque. They both have very few members, but all of them have very high qualifications. There are also 'experts comptables' who are the professional accountants of Belgium.

There are two forms of companies:

SA (Société Anonyme) — public company
SPRL (Société de personnes à responsabilité limitée) — private company

Business is also conducted through partnerships:

SNC (Société en nom collectif) — general unlimited partnership

SCS (Société en commandite simple) — limited partnership

In Belgium the banks are dominant in controlling majority shareholdings in companies. The private investor has much less scope for ownership in public companies.

All companies and partnerships must appoint an auditor (commissaire). Where the company has raised funds from the public there must be a Reviseur d'Entreprise appointed (commissaire reviseur). There are no formal standards of accounting or audit practice in Belgium, and the 'Code de Commerce' provides the basis for reporting requirements. As a result of this there tends to be little useful information provided in a set of annual accounts. The Collège National des Experts Comptables de Belgique have recommended a standard account layout, 'le Plan Comptable', but this is having little impact as yet, though it is likely that the government will introduce legislation providing for more complete financial disclosure by companies. The stock exchange has not demanded any specific information from companies beyond what is normally required under the Code de Commerce. There is some sign that public companies are providing more information in their reports than is required under the Code de Commerce, but private companies' reports are of little practical use as they normally do not:

— disclose sales revenue
— show comparative cost of sales
— display extraordinary items that affect profit for the year
— compile group accounts

Directors of companies are expected to provide an annual Balance Sheet containing:

— fixed assets (valeurs immobilisées)

— current assets: inventory (valeurs d'exploitation)
debtors (comptes de clients)
cash
— capital reserves (capital réserves)
— Long/medium-term liabilities (dettes à long et moyen terme)
— short-term liabilities (dettes à court terme)
— profit to be distributed (bénéfice de l'exercice)

A Profit and Loss Account should contain income and expenditure for the year to provide a net profit (bénéfice net).

The development of European accounting standards and general harmonisation of European practices should improve the presentation of Belgian financial information.

2. *France*

In France there are two major types of company organisation:

SA (Société Anonyme) — public company
SARL (Société à Responsabilité Limitée) — private company

The 'Plan Comptable' provides a detailed statement of financial reporting requirements. There are few large professional accounting firms in France, and as a result of small firms or sole practitioners doing much of the work there has been some concern as to the adequacy and accuracy of some audit work.

Companies must present a Trading Account, Profit and Loss Account and Balance Sheet, but these tend to be produced with tax implications in mind rather than financial disclosure. There is little attempt to provide full notes for a complete appreciation of the financial figures, and it is not unusual to find comparative figures for previous years missing.

From July 1971 quoted companies have been required to provide a consolidated set of accounts, and this has improved the availability of relevant financial information. The

accounts must be consistent — or inconsistencies highlighted — from year to year, and a statement must be
prepared showing net profit and other financial information
on all companies for the previous five years where this is
possible.

Inventory is valued at cost or net realisable value with
FIFO or average cost allowed but not LIFO.

Companies are required to set aside 5% of annual after-tax
profit to a special reserve until this reaches 10% of issued
capital.

3. Federal Republic of Germany

There are two types of companies commonly found in
Germany:

AG (Aktiengesellschaft) — public company
GmbH (Gesellschaft mit beschränkter Haftung) — private
  company

The basis for accounting procedures is set out in the 1965
Public Corporation Law (Aktiengesetz) and the Commercial
Code (Handelsgesetzbuch). These allow a common reporting
system in the country, and are backed by recommendations
from the German Institute of Accountants (Institut der
Wirtschaftsprüfer) which members are expected to follow.
There are no special accounting requirements required by the
stock exchange in Germany.

It is possible, and quite common, for companies to create
'hidden reserves' in their accounts as a result of depreciation
policies and inventory write-downs which are allowed under
German tax legislation.

Companies report in a standard form, but with few notes
or explanations on the figures presented, and exceptional
items are often not disclosed.

Consolidated accounts are prepared, but not on a common
basis — from company to company — and do not include
foreign subsidiaries. Goodwill is written off to retained profit
within five years.

It is not possible to revalue fixed assets, and so these are
shown at cost less accumulated depreciation.

Uncalled share capital is shown as an asset in the Balance Sheet of companies, showing the remaining claim the company has on shareholders. Public companies must set aside 5% of their after-tax profit into a special reserve until this reaches 10% of share capital.

4. *Italy*

There are two major types of companies to be found in Italy:

SPA (Società per Azioni) — public companies
SRL (Società Responsabilità Limitata) — private company

There are also partnerships:

SNC (Società in Nome Collettivo) — general partnership
SAPA (Società in Accomandita per Azioni) — limited partnership with shares
SAS (Società in Accomandita Semplice) — limited partnership

Co-operatives are also to be found (SCRL and SCRIL for limited and unlimited liability).

Directors are elected by shareholders for up to three-year periods and called 'amministratori'. Directors may be charged with bad management and must lodge the lower of 2% of share capital or 200,000 lire (approx. £150) as security in the form of a charge on the company's shares.

The Italian auditors have no formal accounting/auditing standards, and an auditor is not required to pronounce on the fairness of reporting presentation in the annual accounts: it merely states that they comply with Italian law.

The Civil Code sets out the requirements for record-keeping by companies, and the general basis for valuation of assets and liabilities. The major headings in the Balance Sheet are also set out in the Civil Code. A reasonable standard of accounts has been developed which show the assets (attivo) and liabilities (passivo) of the company, together with income (ricavi) and net income (utile netto). However, there is often little consistency adopted, nor any requirement to record changes in accounting treatment of items. Consolidated accounts are not required, and so are rarely available.

Companies must set aside at least 5% of their after-tax profits into a special reserve until this reaches 20% of issued capital.

5. *The Netherlands*

There are two major types of companies in the Netherlands:

NV (Naamloze Vennootschap) — public company
BV (Besloten Vennootschap) — private company

There are also several forms of partnership:

CVOA (Commanditaire Vennootschap op Andelen) — limited with shares
CV (Commanditaire Vennootschap) — limited
VOF (Vennootschap onder Firma) — general partnership
M (Maatschap) — civil partnership.

Legislation lays down the basis for financial reporting in the Act on Financial Statements and through the Netherlands Commercial Code. Companies are expected to 'show a true and fair view' of their financial position and the results for the year, and the statements must be drawn up under acceptable accounting principles with disclosure as to the method of valuation and with consistency and comparative figures from the previous year.

Professional accountants are members of the Nederlands Instituut van Register-accountants with the majority working in six major accounting firms. Accounting standards are high in the Netherlands, and companies provide financial statements for their shareholders on a full and consistent basis. Most companies, where it is applicable, present consolidated accounts or separate statements relating to subsidiary companies.

Fixed assets are normally shown at cost less accumulated depreciation, and revaluation is allowed where there is a capital reserve created. Depreciation on revalued assets is not acceptable to the tax authorities, who otherwise allow all reasonable commercial bases for depreciating assets.

Inventory is valued at cost or net realisable value and most methods of cost valuations are allowed. Companies must split the overall inventory figure into its constituent parts — raw materials, work-in-progress and finished goods — in their financial statements.

6. *European Accounting Standards*

The EEC has commenced work on the harmonisation of company law and the standardisation of accounting practice and reporting for all companies operating in the member countries, and this will continue over the next few years.

Directives have been provided (or drafted) which cover the publication of information, the formation and merging of companies, and the consolidation of subsidiary companies. How far it will be possible to allow a 'true and fair view' approach to providing company information under a standardised system is debatable. This is one of the key factors which concerns U.K. accountants faced with the possibility of having to complete a set of accounts with little or no scope for using their own professional abilities to ensure a sound presentation of the financial information.

Appendix 2: The Imputation System (Advance Corporation Tax)

There have been several changes in the U.K. taxation system for companies. The most recently introduced is that of Advance Corporation Tax (ACT), and this is outlined here to assist understanding of companies' financial statements.

The new system of corporation tax applies to companies making dividend payments to shareholders. Where a company does not make any distribution to shareholders, then all profits will be taxed at the normal rate of corporation tax for the year in question. Where a company pays a dividend to shareholders it will at the same time pay Advance Corporation Tax on the dividend distributed. ACT is calculated as a fraction of the sum distributed, and at present this fraction is three-sevenths. An example will illustrate this procedure:

> X Ltd makes a taxable profit of £50,000 for the year, and pays a dividend of £14,000 to shareholders.

> ACT will be payable of £6,000 (three-sevenths of £14,000)

The £6,000 is paid to the Collector of Taxes at the end of the quarter in which the payment is made. The amount of ACT is then allowed to be set against the normal corporation tax bill of the company:

Corporations tax of	£25,000	is due (assuming a 50% tax rate)
Deduct ACT paid	£6,000	
Tax due to be paid	£19,000	

The fraction which will be applied to calculate ACT will be varied by the government as necessary. The level of three-sevenths was initially chosen to provide the net equivalent of a 30% charge on pre-tax (or gross) income. Thus, if a company made a £700 distribution it would pay £300 ACT, which is the equivalent of 30% on the gross amount (£700 plus £300). The level of 30% equals the basic rate of income tax for 1973—4, and as this basic rate changes so will the fraction used to calculate ACT.

When the dividend is paid to the shareholder it is assumed he received the gross amount. Thus, if the £700 dividend mentioned above were paid to a shareholder of the company, he is assumed for tax purposes to have received this amount gross even though the company has deducted £300 for ACT. The shareholder receives a 'tax credit' for the amount of ACT that has been paid on the dividend (£300) which can be offset against his own tax liability, or claimed back if he has sufficiently low income.

Where a company does not have sufficient corporation tax liability to offset ACT, there are certain provisions in the 1972 Finance Act which apply as follows:

A company has taxable profits of £80,000, £40,000 and £20,000 for three successive years. A dividend of £28,000 is paid in each year. The tax calculations will then be as follows for the first two years:

Year 1

| Corporation tax on profits (50% of £80,000) | £40,000 | |
| ACT paid on dividend | £12,000 | £28,000 |

(three-sevenths of £28,000)

Year 2

| Corporation tax on profits (50% of £40,000) | £20,000 | |
| ACT paid on dividend | £12,000 | £8,000 |

In year 3 the tax due on profits is £10,000 (50% of £20,000) and there has been a payment of £12,000 ACT on the dividend. There is a surplus of ACT in relation to the corporation tax liability of £2,000. However, there is a restriction that the corporation tax bill must be 20% of the taxable profits under these circumstances. That is, £4,000 (20% of £20,000 profit for the year) must be paid in corporation tax. Thus, only £6,000 ACT may be set against the corporation tax liability for the third year.

Year 3

Corporation tax on profits	£10,000	
ACT allowed	£6,000	£4,000

The company may choose under Section 85 of the 1972 Finance Act either to carry back the surplus ACT of £6,000, or to carry it forward to be offset against future tax liabilities.

If the company decided to carry the surplus ACT back, then it could not use it in the second year as the tax liability in that year is just 20% of the taxable profits (20% of £40,000 = £8,000). It must therefore be carried back into the first year to make £22,000 the tax liability in that year (£28,000 − £6,000 ACT). Where corporation tax has already been paid, a repayment will be made to the company. It is not possible to go back further than two years on this basis.

Another form of relief from ACT is available to companies where they have what is termed 'franked investment income'. Franked investment income is produced where one company receives a dividend from another company that has borne ACT.

Company X pays a dividend of £2,000 to company Y

Dividend paid	£1,400	
ACT	£600	£2,000

Company Y has a tax credit of £600 on its investment income of £2,000. When company Y makes a distribution of its own of £2,000:

Dividend	£1,400	
ACT	£600	£2,000

This is termed a 'franked payment' and no ACT is payable by company Y as the tax credit is set against the ACT due on its own dividend.

Appendix 3: VAT and Cash Flow

VAT was introduced into the U.K. on 1 April 1973. This tax is collected at each stage of the production or distribution of goods and services, and borne by the consumer. The introduction of VAT has implications for cash flow planning in all companies. Companies must now consider very carefully the relationship between credit allowed to customers, credit taken from suppliers, and the payment of VAT each quarter to the Customs and Excise. The timing of VAT content of purchases (inputs) and sales (outputs) and the quarterly VAT payments are vital in cash flow forecasting and control for all companies.

Four examples of the impact of VAT on cash flow are provided below. The first two relate to a firm which has a low input/output ratio with VAT of £1,000 being paid on purchases and £5,000 being received from sales for VAT from customers. Payments for the Customs and Excise are made quarterly and amount to £12,000 (three months of VAT on outputs being £15,000 less three months VAT refundable on inputs of £3,000).

Month	VAT paid on purchases	VAT received from sales	VAT paid	Monthly cash flow	Cumulative cash flow
1	—	—	—	—	—
2	(£1,000)	—	—	(£1,000)	(£1,000)
3	(£1,000)	—	—	(£1,000)	(£2,000)
4	(£1,000)	£5,000	(£12,000)	(£8,000)	(£10,000)
5	(£1,000)	£5,000	—	£4,000	(£6,000)
6	(£1,000)	£5,000	—	£4,000	(£2,000)
7	(£1,000)	£5,000	(£12,000)	(£8,000)	(£10,000)

In this example it has been assumed that the firm allows customers three months credit, and takes only one month credit from its suppliers. It can be seen that the cumulative VAT cash flow is continually adverse, reaching a peak of £10,000 when the quarter's VAT is paid. If this situation is reversed so that the firm allows one month to customers but takes three months from suppliers, then the cash flow becomes:

Month	VAT paid on purchases	VAT received from sales	VAT paid	Monthly cash flow	Cumulative cash flow
1	–	–	–	–	–
2	–	£5,000	–	£5,000	£5,000
3	–	£5,000	–	£5,000	£10,000
4	(£1,000)	£5,000	(£12,000)	(£8,000)	£2,000
5	(£1,000)	£5,000	–	£4,000	£6,000
6	(£1,000)	£5,000	–	£4,000	£10,000
7	(£1,000)	£5,000	(£12,000)	(£8,000)	£2,000

The impact of VAT receipts and payments on the cash flow can clearly be seen when the two examples are compared. With the short period of credit taken there is a continuous negative cash flow, whereas when a longer period of credit is taken than is allowed the cash flow is positive.

Where a company has a high VAT input/output ratio the difference in cash flows becomes even greater. In the two examples below it is assumed that £4,000 VAT is paid on materials from suppliers, and £5,000 received from customers for VAT. Payments to the Customs and Excise are made quarterly of £3,000 (three months VAT on sales being £15,000 less three months refundable VAT from purchases of £12,000). The credit allowed in the first example is three months, and that taken one month, and in the second example these are reversed.

Month	VAT paid on purchases	VAT received from sales	VAT paid	Monthly cash flow	Cumulative cash flow
1	–	–	–	–	–
2	(£4,000)	–	–	(£4,000)	(£4,000)
3	(£4,000)	–	–	(£4,000)	(£8,000)
4	(£4,000)	£5,000	(£3,000)	(£2,000)	(£10,000)
5	(£4,000)	£5,000	–	£1,000	(£9,000)
6	(£4,000)	£5,000	–	£1,000	(£8,000)
7	(£4,000)	£5,000	(£3,000)	(£2,000)	(£10,000)

The firm has a high negative cash flow resulting from this situation which means that the payment of VAT, whilst only costing the firm £3,000 each quarter as far as payments to the Customs and Excise are concerned, is requiring a considerable amount of financing if the cumulative cash flow is studied. This highlights the fact that it is not only the size of the VAT payment made that is important to a firm, but also the timing of collection and payment on invoices. The average negative cash flow for this firm will be some £9,000 after month 4, and this must be financed. In the second example it can be seen that the firm has the advantage of additional funds owing to the balance between payment of suppliers and receipts from customers being changed into a more favourable position.

Month	VAT paid on purchases	VAT received from sales	VAT paid	Monthly cash flow	Cumulative cash flow
1	–	–	–	–	–
2	–	£5,000	–	£5,000	£5,000
3	–	£5,000	–	£5,000	£10,000
4	(£4,000)	£5,000	(£3,000)	(£2,000)	£8,000
5	(£4,000)	£5,000	–	£1,000	£9,000
6	(£4,000)	£5,000	–	£1,000	£10,000
7	(£4,000)	£5,000	(£3,000)	(£2,000)	£8,000

Of course, these are extreme and simplified examples, but they illustrate the importance of understanding the impact of VAT on the cash flow of a firm, and show how vital it is to assess the impact of the timing of payment of creditors and receipt of debtors for a firm. Where a company experiences a seasonal change in sales pattern, then the cash situation of the firm may be aggravated by VAT payments, and this must be planned for if effective financing is to be arranged.

Appendix 4: Discount Tables

1

Present value of 1 at compound interest: $(1+r)^{-n}$

YEARS (n)   INTEREST RATES (r)

n	1	2	3	4	5	6	7	8	9	10	11	12	13	14	15	16	17	18	19	20
1	0.9901	0.9804	0.9709	0.9615	0.9524	0.9434	0.9346	0.9259	0.9174	0.9091	0.9009	0.8929	0.8850	0.8772	0.8696	0.8621	0.8547	0.8475	0.8403	0.8333
2	0.9803	0.9612	0.9426	0.9246	0.9070	0.8900	0.8734	0.8573	0.8417	0.8264	0.8116	0.7972	0.7831	0.7695	0.7561	0.7432	0.7305	0.7182	0.7062	0.6944
3	0.9706	0.9423	0.9151	0.8890	0.8638	0.8396	0.8163	0.7938	0.7722	0.7513	0.7312	0.7118	0.6931	0.6750	0.6575	0.6407	0.6244	0.6086	0.5934	0.5787
4	0.9610	0.9238	0.8885	0.8548	0.8227	0.7921	0.7629	0.7350	0.7084	0.6830	0.6587	0.6355	0.6133	0.5921	0.5718	0.5523	0.5337	0.5158	0.4987	0.4823
5	0.9515	0.9057	0.8626	0.8219	0.7835	0.7473	0.7130	0.6806	0.6499	0.6209	0.5935	0.5674	0.5428	0.5194	0.4972	0.4761	0.4561	0.4371	0.4190	0.4019
6	0.9420	0.8880	0.8375	0.7903	0.7462	0.7050	0.6663	0.6302	0.5963	0.5645	0.5346	0.5066	0.4803	0.4556	0.4323	0.4104	0.3898	0.3704	0.3521	0.3349
7	0.9327	0.8706	0.8131	0.7599	0.7107	0.6651	0.6227	0.5835	0.5470	0.5132	0.4817	0.4523	0.4251	0.3996	0.3759	0.3538	0.3332	0.3139	0.2959	0.2791
8	0.9235	0.8535	0.7894	0.7307	0.6768	0.6274	0.5820	0.5403	0.5019	0.4665	0.4339	0.4039	0.3762	0.3506	0.3269	0.3050	0.2848	0.2660	0.2487	0.2326
9	0.9143	0.8368	0.7664	0.7026	0.6446	0.5919	0.5439	0.5002	0.4604	0.4241	0.3909	0.3606	0.3329	0.3075	0.2843	0.2630	0.2434	0.2255	0.2090	0.1938
10	0.9053	0.8203	0.7441	0.6756	0.6139	0.5584	0.5083	0.4632	0.4224	0.3855	0.3522	0.3220	0.2946	0.2697	0.2472	0.2267	0.2080	0.1911	0.1756	0.1615
11	0.8963	0.8043	0.7224	0.6496	0.5847	0.5268	0.4751	0.4289	0.3875	0.3505	0.3173	0.2875	0.2607	0.2366	0.2149	0.1954	0.1778	0.1619	0.1476	0.1346
12	0.8874	0.7885	0.7014	0.6246	0.5568	0.4970	0.4440	0.3971	0.3555	0.3186	0.2858	0.2567	0.2307	0.2076	0.1869	0.1685	0.1520	0.1372	0.1240	0.1122
13	0.8787	0.7730	0.6810	0.6006	0.5303	0.4688	0.4150	0.3677	0.3262	0.2897	0.2575	0.2292	0.2042	0.1821	0.1625	0.1452	0.1299	0.1163	0.1042	0.0935
14	0.8700	0.7579	0.6611	0.5775	0.5051	0.4423	0.3878	0.3405	0.2992	0.2633	0.2320	0.2046	0.1807	0.1597	0.1413	0.1252	0.1110	0.0985	0.0876	0.0779
15	0.8613	0.7430	0.6419	0.5553	0.4810	0.4173	0.3624	0.3152	0.2745	0.2394	0.2090	0.1827	0.1599	0.1401	0.1229	0.1079	0.0949	0.0835	0.0736	0.0649
16	0.8528	0.7284	0.6232	0.5339	0.4581	0.3936	0.3387	0.2919	0.2519	0.2176	0.1883	0.1631	0.1415	0.1229	0.1069	0.0930	0.0811	0.0708	0.0618	0.0541
17	0.8444	0.7142	0.6050	0.5134	0.4363	0.3714	0.3166	0.2703	0.2311	0.1978	0.1696	0.1456	0.1252	0.1078	0.0929	0.0802	0.0693	0.0600	0.0520	0.0451
18	0.8360	0.7002	0.5874	0.4936	0.4155	0.3503	0.2959	0.2502	0.2120	0.1799	0.1528	0.1300	0.1108	0.0946	0.0808	0.0691	0.0592	0.0508	0.0437	0.0376
19	0.8277	0.6864	0.5703	0.4746	0.3957	0.3305	0.2765	0.2317	0.1945	0.1635	0.1377	0.1161	0.0981	0.0829	0.0703	0.0596	0.0506	0.0431	0.0367	0.0313
20	0.8195	0.6730	0.5537	0.4564	0.3769	0.3118	0.2584	0.2145	0.1784	0.1486	0.1240	0.1037	0.0868	0.0728	0.0611	0.0514	0.0433	0.0365	0.0308	0.0261
25	0.7798	0.6095	0.4776	0.3751	0.2953	0.2330	0.1842	0.1460	0.1160	0.0923	0.0736	0.0588	0.0471	0.0378	0.0304	0.0245	0.0197	0.0160	0.0129	0.0105
30	0.7419	0.5521	0.4120	0.3083	0.2314	0.1741	0.1314	0.0994	0.0754	0.0573	0.0437	0.0334	0.0256	0.0196	0.0151	0.0116	0.0090	0.0070	0.0054	0.0042
35	0.7059	0.5000	0.3554	0.2534	0.1813	0.1301	0.0937	0.0676	0.0490	0.0356	0.0259	0.0189	0.0139	0.0102	0.0075	0.0055	0.0041	0.0030	0.0023	0.0017
40	0.6717	0.4529	0.3066	0.2083	0.1420	0.0972	0.0668	0.0460	0.0318	0.0221	0.0154	0.0107	0.0075	0.0053	0.0037	0.0026	0.0019	0.0013	0.0010	0.0007
45	0.6391	0.4102	0.2644	0.1712	0.1113	0.0727	0.0476	0.0313	0.0207	0.0137	0.0091	0.0061	0.0041	0.0027	0.0019	0.0013	0.0009	0.0006	0.0004	0.0003
50	0.6080	0.3715	0.2281	0.1407	0.0872	0.0543	0.0339	0.0213	0.0134	0.0085	0.0054	0.0035	0.0022	0.0014	0.0009	0.0006	0.0004	0.0003	0.0002	0.0001

Present value of an annuity of 1: $\dfrac{1-(1+r)^{-n}}{r}$

YEARS (n)   INTEREST RATES (r)

n	1	2	3	4	5	6	7	8	9	10	11	12	13	14	15	16	17	18
1	0·9901	0·9804	0·9709	0·9615	0·9524	0·9434	0·9346	0·9259	0·9174	0·9091	0·9009	0·8929	0·8850	0·8772	0·8696	0·8621	0·8547	0·8475
2	1·9704	1·9416	1·9135	1·8861	1·8594	1·8334	1·8080	1·7833	1·7591	1·7355	1·7125	1·6901	1·6681	1·6467	1·6257	1·6052	1·5852	1·5656
3	2·9410	2·8839	2·8286	2·7751	2·7232	2·6730	2·6243	2·5771	2·5313	2·4869	2·4437	2·4018	2·3612	2·3216	2·2832	2·2459	2·2096	2·1743
4	3·9020	3·8077	3·7171	3·6299	3·5460	3·4651	3·3872	3·3121	3·2397	3·1699	3·1024	3·0373	2·9745	2·9137	2·8550	2·7982	2·7432	2·6901
5	4·8534	4·7135	4·5797	4·4518	4·3295	4·2124	4·1002	3·9927	3·8897	3·7908	3·6959	3·6048	3·5172	3·4331	3·3522	3·2743	3·1993	3·1272
6	5·7955	5·6014	5·4172	5·2421	5·0757	4·9173	4·7665	4·6229	4·4859	4·3553	4·2305	4·1114	3·9975	3·8887	3·7845	3·6847	3·5892	3·4976
7	6·7282	6·4720	6·2303	6·0021	5·7864	5·5824	5·3893	5·2064	5·0330	4·8684	4·7122	4·5638	4·4226	4·2883	4·1604	4·0386	3·9224	3·8115
8	7·6517	7·3255	7·0197	6·7327	6·4632	6·2098	5·9713	5·7466	5·5348	5·3349	5·1461	4·9676	4·7988	4·6389	4·4873	4·3436	4·2072	4·0776
9	8·5660	8·1622	7·7861	7·4353	7·1078	6·8017	6·5152	6·2469	5·9952	5·7590	5·5370	5·3282	5·1317	4·9464	4·7716	4·6065	4·4506	4·3030
10	9·4713	8·9826	8·5302	8·1109	7·7217	7·3601	7·0236	6·7101	6·4177	6·1446	5·8892	5·6502	5·4262	5·2161	5·0188	4·8332	4·6586	4·4941
11	10·3676	9·7868	9·2526	8·7605	8·3064	7·8869	7·4987	7·1390	6·8052	6·4951	6·2065	5·9377	5·6869	5·4527	5·2337	5·0286	4·8364	4·6560
12	11·2551	10·5753	9·9540	9·3851	8·8633	8·3838	7·9427	7·5361	7·1607	6·8137	6·4924	6·1944	5·9176	5·6603	5·4206	5·1971	4·9884	4·7932
13	12·1337	11·3484	10·6350	9·9856	9·3936	8·8527	8·3577	7·9038	7·4869	7·1034	6·7499	6·4235	6·1218	5·8424	5·5831	5·3423	5·1183	4·9095
14	13·0037	12·1062	11·2961	10·5631	9·8986	9·2950	8·7455	8·2442	7·7862	7·3667	6·9819	6·6282	6·3025	6·0021	5·7245	5·4675	5·2293	5·0081
15	13·8651	12·8493	11·9379	11·1184	10·3797	9·7122	9·1079	8·5595	8·0607	7·6061	7·1909	6·8109	6·4624	6·1422	5·8474	5·5755	5·3242	5·0916
16	14·7179	13·5777	12·5611	11·6523	10·8378	10·1059	9·4466	8·8514	8·3126	7·8237	7·3792	6·9740	6·6039	6·2651	5·9542	5·6685	5·4053	5·1624
17	15·5623	14·2919	13·1661	12·1657	11·2741	10·4773	9·7632	9·1216	8·5436	8·0216	7·5488	7·1196	6·7291	6·3729	6·0472	5·7487	5·4746	5·2223
18	16·3983	14·9920	13·7535	12·6593	11·6896	10·8276	10·0591	9·3719	8·7556	8·2014	7·7016	7·2497	6·8399	6·4674	6·1280	5·8178	5·5339	5·2732
19	17·2260	15·6785	14·3238	13·1339	12·0853	11·1581	10·3356	9·6036	8·9501	8·3649	7·8393	7·3658	6·9380	6·5504	6·1982	5·8775	5·5845	5·3162
20	18·0456	16·3514	14·8775	13·5903	12·4622	11·4699	10·5940	9·8181	9·1285	8·5136	7·9633	7·4694	7·0248	6·6231	6·2593	5·9288	5·6278	5·3527
25	22·0232	19·5235	17·4131	15·6221	14·0939	12·7834	11·6536	10·6748	9·8226	9·0770	8·4217	7·8431	7·3300	6·8729	6·4641	6·0971	5·7662	5·4669
30	25·8077	22·3965	19·6004	17·2920	15·3725	13·7648	12·4090	11·2578	10·2737	9·4269	8·6938	8·0552	7·4957	7·0027	6·5660	6·1772	5·8294	5·5168
35	29·4086	24·9986	21·4872	18·6646	16·3742	14·4982	12·9477	11·6546	10·5668	9·6442	8·8552	8·1755	7·5856	7·0700	6·6166	6·2153	5·8582	5·5386
40	32·8347	27·3555	23·1148	19·7928	17·1591	15·0463	13·3317	11·9246	10·7574	9·7791	8·9511	8·2438	7·6344	7·1050	6·6418	6·2335	5·8713	5·5482
45	36·0945	29·4902	24·5187	20·7200	17·7741	15·4558	13·6055	12·1084	10·8812	9·8628	9·0079	8·2825	7·6609	7·1232	6·6543	6·2421	5·8773	5·5523
50	39·1961	31·4236	25·7298	21·4822	18·2559	15·7619	13·8007	12·2335	10·9617	9·9148	9·0417	8·3045	7·6752	7·1327	6·6605	6·2463	5·8801	5·5541

Index

Budgetary control (*cont.*)
  definition, 175
  and key factors, 176-7
  participation, 180
  PPBS, 189
  reporting, 181
  zero-base, 189
Budgeting
  cash, 81-7, 179
  and company objectives, 171
  effective, 178
  flexible, 186-7
  process, 175-81
Business finance *see* Sources of finance

Capital
  cost of, 122
  equity, 97
  fixed, 98
  gearing, 100-2
  investment appraisal, 111-29
  share premium account, 64
  shareholders funds, 22, 23
  venture, 95
  and voting rights, 98
  working, 23
Capitalisation rate *see* Stock exchange ratios, earnings-yield
Caplan, E. H., 188
Cash budgeting, 81-7, 179
Cash-flow
  and planning, 174
  and taxation, 119
  timing of, 115
Chairman's statement, 28, 29
Chandler *v.* Crane Christmas & Co. (1951), 11
Companies Acts (1948, 1967), 24, 27-9
  and stock, 43
Contribution analysis
  applications, 162-4
  and decision making, 165-7
  divisional performance, 167
  formula, 159-61
  margin of safety, 161
  marginal, direct, variable costing, 162
  and overhead allocation, 148-50
  pricing policy, 164, 167-8
Convertible preference shares, 99
Corporate personality, 3
Corporate planning, objectives, 171-5

Cost
  allocation, 150
  classification, 130-5
  and control, 130
  replacement, 5, 38
  unit, 150
Cost of capital, 122
Costing techniques
  absorption, 135
  contract, 147
  full *see* absorption
  marginal, direct, variable *see* Contribution analysis
  process, 146-7
  standard, 137-44, 145
Costs
  cost-volume-profit analysis, 154
  direct and indirect, 132
  fixed and variable, 133-4
  overheads, 136
  product and period, 135
  semi-fixed and semi-variable, 135
  total, 134
Credit, taken, 21
Credit policy, and cash budgeting, 87
Creditors, preferential, 3
Credits, 21
Cumulative difference graph, 185
Cumulative preference shares, 99
Current liabilities *see* Liabilities, current
Current purchasing power, 38-42

Debentures
  convertible, 99
  fixed, 99
  floating, 99
Debits, 21
Debtors, 48
Depreciation
  accumulated, 33
  historic cost, 5
  reducing-balance, 35
  straight-line, 34
  sum-of-the-digits, 35
Direct costing *see* Contribution analysis
Directors' report, 27
Discounted cash flow (DCF), 119
Discounting, 115-18
Dividends, 50
Double-entry accounting, 11-21